Crime

DATE DUE

10-24-06	
11-9-06	
2-1-10	

Other Books in the Current Controversies Series:

The Abortion Controversy
Alcoholism
Computers and Society
The Disabled
Drug Trafficking
Energy Alternatives
Ethics
Europe
Family Violence
Gambling
Garbage and Waste
Gay Rights
Genetics and Intelligence
Gun Control
Hate Crimes
Hunger
Illegal Drugs
Illegal Immigration
The Information Highway
Interventionism
Iraq
Marriage and Divorce
Minorities
Nationalism and Ethnic Conflict
Native American Rights
Police Brutality
Politicians and Ethics
Pollution
Reproductive Technologies
Sexual Harassment
Smoking
Teen Addiction
Urban Terrorism
Violence Against Women
Violence in the Media
Women in the Military
Youth Violence

Crime

David Bender, *Publisher*
Bruno Leone, *Executive Editor*

Brenda Stalcup, *Managing Editor*
Scott Barbour, *Senior Editor*

Paul A. Winters, *Book Editor*

CURRENT CONTROVERSIES

Cover photo: Nina Berman/SIPA Press

Library of Congress Cataloging-in-Publication Data

Crime / Paul A. Winters, book editor.
     p. cm. — (Current controversies)
    Includes bibliographical references and index.
    ISBN 1-56510-686-5 (pbk.). — ISBN 1-56510-687-3
(lib. : alk. paper)
    1. Criminology—United States. 2. Crime—United States. 3. Criminal Justice, Administration of—United States. I. Winters, Paul A., 1965–   .
II. Series.
HV6789.C6813   1998
364'.0973—dc21   97-27793
                                                CIP

© 1998 by Greenhaven Press, Inc., PO Box 289009, San Diego, CA 92198-9009
Printed in the U.S.A.

Contents

Chapter 1: What Causes Crime?

Chapter 2: Is Crime Increasing?

Chapter 3: Can Stronger Criminal Justice Measures Prevent Crime?

prevention measures, such as drug treatment, gun control laws, and alternative sentencing, are less costly and more effective at preventing crime.

Chapter 4: How Can Juvenile Crime Be Prevented?

future teen crime wave rests on the faulty assumption that a fixed percentage of all future teenagers will engage in criminal activity. Further, there is no reason to believe that future teenagers will be more violent than teens today.

Politicians, the media, and some criminology experts predict a future teenage crime wave; however, the truth is that increases in violent crime rates are mainly the result of adult violence directed against children. This increase in adult violence most likely stems from the rise in adult drug abuse.

Foreword

By definition, controversies are "discussions of questions in which opposing opinions clash" (Webster's Twentieth Century Dictionary Unabridged). Few would deny that controversies are a pervasive part of the human condition and exist on virtually every level of human enterprise. Controversies transpire between individuals and among groups, within nations and between nations. Controversies supply the grist necessary for progress by providing challenges and challengers to the status quo. They also create atmospheres where strife and warfare can flourish. A world without controversies would be a peaceful world; but it also would be, by and large, static and prosaic.

The Series' Purpose

The purpose of the Current Controversies series is to explore many of the social, political, and economic controversies dominating the national and international scenes today. Titles selected for inclusion in the series are highly focused and specific. For example, from the larger category of criminal justice, Current Controversies deals with specific topics such as police brutality, gun control, white collar crime, and others. The debates in Current Controversies also are presented in a useful, timeless fashion. Articles and book excerpts included in each title are selected if they contribute valuable, long-range ideas to the overall debate. And wherever possible, current information is enhanced with historical documents and other relevant materials. Thus, while individual titles are current in focus, every effort is made to ensure that they will not become quickly outdated. Books in the Current Controversies series will remain important resources for librarians, teachers, and students for many years.

In addition to keeping the titles focused and specific, great care is taken in the editorial format of each book in the series. Book introductions and chapter prefaces are offered to provide background material for readers. Chapters are organized around several key questions that are answered with diverse opinions representing all points on the political spectrum. Materials in each chapter include opinions in which authors clearly disagree as well as alternative opinions in which authors may agree on a broader issue but disagree on the possible solutions. In this way, the content of each volume in Current Controversies mirrors the mosaic of opinions encountered in society. Readers will quickly realize that there are many viable answers to these complex issues. By questioning each author's conclusions, students and casual readers can begin to develop the critical thinking skills so important to evaluating opinionated material.

Current Controversies is also ideal for controlled research. Each anthology in the series is composed of primary sources taken from a wide gamut of informational categories including periodicals, newspapers, books, United States and foreign government documents, and the publications of private and public organizations. Readers will find factual support for reports, debates, and research papers covering all areas of important issues. In addition, an annotated table of contents, an index, a book and periodical bibliography, and a list of organizations to contact are included in each book to expedite further research.

Perhaps more than ever before in history, people are confronted with diverse and contradictory information. During the Persian Gulf War, for example, the public was not only treated to minute-to-minute coverage of the war, it was also inundated with critiques of the coverage and countless analyses of the factors motivating U.S. involvement. Being able to sort through the plethora of opinions accompanying today's major issues, and to draw one's own conclusions, can be a complicated and frustrating struggle. It is the editors' hope that Current Controversies will help readers with this struggle.

Greenhaven Press anthologies primarily consist of previously published material taken from a variety of sources, including periodicals, books, scholarly journals, newspapers, government documents, and position papers from private and public organizations. These original sources are often edited for length and to ensure their accessibility for a young adult audience. The anthology editors also change the original titles of these works in order to clearly present the main thesis of each viewpoint and to explicitly indicate the opinion presented in the viewpoint. These alterations are made in consideration of both the reading and comprehension levels of a young adult audience. Every effort is made to ensure that Greenhaven Press accurately reflects the original intent of the authors included in this anthology.

"There are far more murders, rapes, and robberies by young people than in the past."

Margaret O. Hyde

"The vast majority of juveniles arrested in America are arrested for property crimes and other less serious offenses—not crimes of violence."

Michael A. Jones and Barry Krisberg

Introduction

Crime statistics compiled by the FBI in its yearly crime index show what many in the law enforcement field consider to be an encouraging trend. From 1990 to 1995, the crime rate declined steadily in every category: murders, rapes, assaults, robberies, burglaries, and thefts. Sociologists and criminologists debate the explanation for this downward turn in crime rates; improved economic conditions and tougher criminal justice measures are two of the theories offered. Other experts, however, dispute whether the decline is significant, pointing out that crime rates in many categories are still higher than in the mid-1980s. These scholars also deny that the trend of decreasing crime rates will continue.

James Alan Fox, dean of the College of Criminal Justice at Northeastern University in Boston, is among those who believe that the recent drop in crime rates is merely the lull before an approaching crime storm. The reason for the current decrease in crime, he maintains, is the demographic dip in the number of teenage and young adult males (ages fourteen to twenty-five), the part of the population most likely to commit crimes. In addition, he points out that even as the overall rate has decreased, the crime rate among the present population of teenaged males has grown, and many of their crimes are more violent and vicious in nature than those committed by young males of preceding generations. As the numbers of teenaged males increase in the near future (a demographic certainty), he predicts, the crime rate will naturally return to previous levels and will possibly climb even higher.

Expanding upon Fox's argument, Princeton University professor John J. DiIulio Jr. argues that it is more than simply the number of boys approaching their crime-prone teen years that portends an impending explosion in the crime rate. In his opinion, it is the moral poverty in which the next generation of adolescents is being raised that bodes ill for the nation's crime rates. Moral poverty, according to DiIulio, is "the poverty of growing up surrounded by deviant, delinquent, and criminal adults in abusive, violence-ridden, fatherless, Godless, and jobless settings."

According to DiIulio, research shows that a small proportion of juvenile criminals is responsible for nearly half of all offenses committed by all teenagers. What is well established yet little known, he asserts, is that each successive generation of this segment of young offenders is approximately three times more violent and dangerous than the previous one. In DiIulio's view, this is because each generation grows up "in more extreme conditions of moral poverty than the one before it." The criminal behavior of the current population of offenders brings about the social conditions to produce an even more deviant future breed of juvenile "superpredators," he maintains. Today's criminals are frightening, in DiIulio's opinion, because they have never learned right from wrong, they have no concept of the relationship between present actions and future consequences, and they place no value on the lives of others. But tomorrow's superpredators are destined to be worse, he contends, because they are being raised in the fatherless families and drug- and violence-ridden neighborhoods created by today's criminals. And due to current population trends, he adds, there will be more of these juvenile criminals in the near future.

Many criminologists, however, disagree with the predictions of Fox and DiIulio. Among them, Alfred Blumstein, a professor of urban systems at Carnegie Mellon University in Pittsburgh, remains unconvinced that a juvenile crime wave is imminent. Blumstein contends that crime rates do not follow demographic trends in the numbers of teenage males as closely as proponents of the crime wave theory believe. He argues that violent crime has increased among the current population of teenagers (even though that population is relatively small) due to the influence of the drug trade and a lack of economic opportunity. As the economy improves and drug battles diminish, Blumstein maintains, fewer young people will become involved in crime. Counter to the beliefs of Fox and others, he predicts that crime rates will continue their downward slide.

Others dispute DiIulio's theory of a coming generation of superpredators. University of California, Berkeley professor Jerome H. Skolnick, for one, asserts that DiIulio's theory of moral poverty "ignores such factors as racism, joblessness, inequality, and poverty." Although there undoubtedly will be more teenagers in the near future, he contends, whether they become incorrigibly violent depends on how society addresses these root causes of crime.

Skolnick argues that poverty and unemployment within urban neighborhoods historically have been "a recipe for the emergence of youth cultures leading to rising crime rates." He cites research by sociologists Kenneth Land, David Cantor, and Stephen Russell that shows a long-term correlation between unemployment rates and property crime rates, particularly within inner cities. In Skolnick's opinion, this research suggests that long-term economic deprivation is a motivation to commit crime. Isolated by declining economic conditions and racial divisions, he contends, urban neighborhoods over the years have developed patterns of lawlessness and family instability. As further proof, Skolnick points out that the declining crime rates of the 1990s have been accompanied by declining unemployment rates. It is by no means certain, he concludes, that America is on the brink of a wave of juvenile crime and violence.

Debates about future crime trends are inextricably interwoven with arguments about juvenile crime, since many believe that today's juvenile delinquents are destined to become tomorrow's adult felons. *Crime: Current Controversies* presents debates about crime rates, juvenile crime, and other topics in these chapters: What Causes Crime? Is Crime Increasing? Can Stronger Criminal Justice Measures Prevent Crime? How Can Juvenile Crime Be Prevented? The issues surrounding crime are controversial and, as the viewpoints that follow demonstrate, reasonable people can draw differing conclusions from the available evidence.

Chapter 1

What Causes Crime?

Chapter Preface

Though crimes occur everywhere, high rates of crime—along with jobless-ness, illegitimacy, and poverty—are concentrated in inner cities. Social scien-tists therefore look for the causes of crime in the correlations between these so-cial factors.

Like many liberals, Samuel L. Myers, the Roy Wilkins Professor of Human Relations and Social Justice at the University of Minnesota, maintains that eco-nomic factors (such as joblessness and poverty) are the root causes of crime. He argues that the decline of industry in cities and the resultant loss of stable, well-paying jobs, particularly for black men, "contribute to blocked opportunities, creating incentives to illegal activity." He maintains that the majority of inner-city youth can earn more money from illegal activities such as drug dealing than from the few legitimate minimum-wage jobs available. Because a lack of economic opportunities leads to crime and, ultimately, imprisonment for so many blacks, Myers continues, the number of "marriageable" black men in in-ner cities is at a critically low level, contributing to the illegitimacy and destabi-lized families that conservatives say are the causes of crime.

Like most conservatives, however, David Rubenstein, professor of sociology at the University of Illinois at Chicago, rejects the argument that economic fac-tors cause crime. "It is hard to see crimes such as rape, drug use and most homicides and assaults as substitutes for employment," he asserts. Citing data compiled from 1930 to 1990, he maintains that there is no correlation between unemployment rates and crime rates. He points out that the number of single-parent families within a community is more strongly correlated with the crime rate than are racial makeup or income levels. The true cause of crime, in Rubenstein's opinion, is the culture within America's inner cities that promotes illegitimacy, welfare dependency, and other social pathologies.

While conservatives look at social factors to find the cause of crime, liberals contend that economic factors are to blame. These divergent views are reflected in the following chapter on the causes of crime.

Social Factors Cause Crime

by Ed Rubenstein

About the author: *Ed Rubenstein is the economics analyst for* National Review.

Polls show that Americans regard crime as the number one social problem facing the nation. We fear being a victim of violent crime, or having our property violated, far more than we fear being unemployed or suffering a loss of income. Crime far outstrips inflation, the deficit, or any other economic problem. Yet until recently, the economics profession had little to say about the root causes of criminal activity. Economists could do little more than tally the figures. We know, for example, that there were about 34 million criminal acts committed in the United States in 1992—about 94,000 crimes daily. This is a Justice Department estimate. We don't know the exact number, because many, if not most, crimes are not reported.

We do know, however, that the national crime rate—crimes per capita—has tripled over the past 30 years. And at least 71 percent of all violent crimes (rape, robbery, assault, personal theft) involve some kind of economic loss. The direct costs in one sample year, 1992—in cash, cars, and personal property—came to about $18 billion. But this is merely the tip of the iceberg. Crime victims suffer trauma, depression, and fear that inevitably affect their ability to work and help others. These problems can last a lifetime. The total costs to crime victims can, therefore, easily reach $250 billion to $500 billion each year.

Then there are the public costs. State and local governments spend about $80 billion per year on public safety. That includes police, courts, prisons, and parole systems. There are about 700,000 policemen and an even larger number of private security guards. We have, in effect, become a police state, incarcerating 1.1 million people. Our incarceration rate has doubled since 1980. It is the world's highest—4 times greater than Canada's, 5 times England's, 14 times Japan's.

From Ed Rubenstein, "The Economics of Crime," *Imprimis*, August 1995; ©1995. Reprinted by permission of *Imprimis*, the monthly journal of Hillsdale College.

The Causes of Crime

How to explain the exploding crime rate? Economists are at a loss. Most economic activities are rational. The decision to buy a car, a house, or to go to college, for example, is usually the result of careful calculations. Costs are weighed against benefits. By contrast, criminal activity seems irrational.

The career criminal, according to James Q. Wilson, was long ago identified as: "typically an impulsive young man who grew up in a discordant family where one or both parents had a criminal record, discipline was erratic, and human relations were cold and unpredictable. He had a low IQ and poor verbal skills. His behavioral problems appeared early, often by age eight, and included dishonesty and aggressiveness. Even in kindergarten or first grade he was disruptive, defiant, and badly behaved. He had few friends and was not emotionally close to those associates with whom he began stealing and assaulting."

These social pathologies are not the things economists feel comfortable talking about, at least not professionally. We like to quantify things. We use prices and incomes to explain behavior. Anti-social attitudes don't fit into our economic "models." Indeed, the notion that economic factors alone explain crime doesn't jibe with the facts. Real per capita incomes have doubled since 1960. That should have substantially reduced the crime rate. The male unemployment rate is lower now than it was then. So is the poverty rate. The percentage of people who are church members is about the same. Church attendance rates are higher.

> *"The notion that economic factors alone explain crime doesn't jibe with the facts."*

But look closely. The crime rate is increasingly concentrated in the inner city. You are actually *less* likely to be assaulted, raped, robbed, or burglarized today than you were in 1980—unless you are a minority resident of an inner-city neighborhood. For the white middle class, all crime rates except auto theft are down.

But the fear of crime is universal even if the actuality is local. For minorities, rates of all crimes, including homicide, are up. Black males living in these areas are 10 times more likely to die violently than the average American. And inner-city blacks also suffer much higher rates of rape, robbery, burglary, and aggravated assault than do whites.

This is not about race, nor about economics. Yes, the gap between the rich and the poor, who are often minorities, has widened over the past three decades. But our "poor" are the envy of poor people in every other nation in the world. Most countries have far wider income dispersions, along with far lower crime rates.

Illegitimacy Is a Root Cause of Crime

Social factors, especially the alarming decline in intact families, explain most of the rise of criminality. The percentage of black children born to single mothers has increased from 22 percent in 1960 to *68 percent* today. In inner cities, the figure is typically in excess of *80 percent*. And the newest trend is white illegitimacy, which has exploded from 2 percent in 1960 to *22 percent* today.

> *"Social factors, especially the alarming decline in intact families, explain most of the rise of criminality."*

Using sophisticated statistical models, economists have at last begun measuring the impact of family dissolution on crime. In 1994, William Niskanen, chairman of the Cato Institute, reported that a 1 percentage point increase in births to single mothers appears to increase the violent crime rate by 1.7 percent. Obviously, the babies themselves aren't committing the crimes. Illegitimacy is merely a proxy for a general decline in moral values and attitudes toward authority. Similarly, Niskanen found that a 1 percent rise in the black or Hispanic population pushes the violent crime rate up by about 1.8 percent.

Single parent families, and the culture that condones them, are the root cause of most violent crimes. As Charles Murray wrote recently in the *Wall Street Journal*, "Illegitimacy is the single most important social problem of our time—more important than crime, drugs, poverty, illiteracy, welfare, or homelessness because it drives everything else." We do not have the highest illegitimacy rate in the world. Sweden does. Yet crime is not a major problem there. The U.S. differs from the permissive welfare states of Western Europe in having an underclass that is not merely poor, but has few chances of escaping poverty. The inner-city poor are isolated in areas where not working is the norm, crime is commonplace, and welfare is a way of life.

Because the "underclass" is not a census category, we don't know for sure how much crime it causes. But we do know that most crimes are committed by repeat offenders. People who once agreed that the cause of poverty and crime was a lack of money—and the solution was more money—now admit that, at least for the underclass, the problem is not simply money; it is behavior.

The Rational Criminal

If the war against crime depended on our changing this behavior, the prospect would be grim indeed. Such attitudes do not change very rapidly. If attitudes change slowly, then short-run changes in crime rates must reflect something else—perhaps changes in the opportunities or incentives facing criminals.

About 25 years ago, economists began developing a new model of criminal activity. The major breakthrough was the work of Gary Becker, a University of Chicago economist and now a Nobel laureate. In Becker's model, criminals are rational individuals acting in their own self interest. In deciding to commit a crime, criminals weigh the expected costs against the expected benefits. The "cost" of crime to criminals consists of two parts. One is the income foregone by devoting time to criminal activity—the so-called opportunity cost. For most criminals this is very small. They usually are unskilled and uneducated. Legal alternatives usually don't pay as well.

The second, and far larger, cost is the time criminals expect to be incarcerated because of their activity. "Expected punishment" is not the same as the length of time a convicted criminal actually spends in prison. Most crimes never result in an arrest. Many of those arrested aren't prosecuted. Many convicts are paroled. Expected punishment, from the criminal's viewpoint, is a probability, not a certainty.

Take burglary. Only 7 percent of U.S. burglaries result in an arrest according to the National Center for Policy Analysis (NCPA). Of those arrested, 87 percent are prosecuted. Of those prosecuted, 79 percent are convicted. Of those convicted, a mere 25 percent are sent to prison. (Most are paroled.) After multiplying these probabilities, we see that a potential burglar faces only a 1.2 percent chance of going to prison for each act of burglary committed. Once in prison, he will stay there for about 13 months. But since he will escape imprisonment more than 98 percent of the time, the expected "cost" of each burglary to the burglar is only 4.8 days.

The rational criminal will ask himself whether an act of burglary is likely to net him goods worth more than 4.8 days behind bars. If the answer is yes, then his crime pays.

The goal of the criminal justice system is to raise expected costs of crime to criminals above the expected benefits. People will commit crimes only so long as they are willing to pay the prices society "charges." Unfortunately, the expected prices of criminal activity are shockingly low. In 1990, a murderer could expect to spend only 1.8 years of his life in prison for his crime. A rapist could expect just 60 days. A car thief, 1.5 days. If the numbers appear low, the reality is worse. Those crimes with the longest expected prison terms (murder, rape, robbery, and assault) are the least frequently committed, comprising about 12 percent of all serious crime. The remaining 88 percent carry an expected prison term of only a few days.

Despite the enormous rise in criminal justice spending since 1950, the "cost" of crime to the average criminal is lower today. Again, we can look at the figures from the NCPA: Between 1950 and 1974, the expected punishment for all serious crimes fell from 24 days to 5.5 days. The crime rate rose 300 percent over this period. Obviously, criminals themselves were aware of the reduction in expected

> *"Single parent families, and the culture that condones them, are the root cause of most violent crimes."*

punishment. They responded to the reduced "cost" of crime by producing more of it. Similarly, during the 1980s, Congress created mandatory minimum sentences for certain violent crimes, urging the states to do likewise. As expected time in prison rose, the crime rate declined. Once again, criminals responded rationally to economic incentives.

Numerous crime bills have tried to increase the costs and reduce the economic incentives to criminal activity. Despite spending enormous sums—$30 billion authorized in the 1994 crime bill alone—they generally have missed their target. For example, the 1994 bill authorized federal grants to hire 100,000 new police officers. However, no funds were made available for the woefully overburdened court system. Thus while arrest rates may go up, the probability of prosecution will fall, leaving the expected "cost" of crime about where it was before. Worse still, political considerations dictated the dispersal of funds: at least half of all the new police funds were directed to cities with populations under 150,000.

Fighting Crime Effectively

Although crime is a national problem, it is best fought by local initiatives. Unfortunately, Congress doesn't see it that way. The 1994 bill is laden with federal micromanagement. And keeping career criminals off the street is essential to fighting crime. "Three strikes and you're out" is a good start, but it's expensive. Maintaining a single criminal behind bars costs taxpayers at least $25,000 per year. However, the Rand Corporation reports that the average professional criminal commits between 187 and 287 crimes a year, at a cost to society of $2,300 per crime—more than $400,000 a year. So paying for new prisons is really a bargain.

> *"Despite the enormous rise in criminal justice spending since 1950, the 'cost' of crime to the average criminal is lower today."*

Yet we must remember that the ultimate cause of criminal activity is a breakdown in internal controls—call it character or personal morality. Some people simply never learn the difference between right and wrong. Public policy cannot directly change the internal controls on which human character, and ultimately human behavior, depend. But the criminal justice system can perform the essential role of reminding society that crime is wrong and that it carries serious consequences.

Economic Factors Cause Crime

by *New Unionist*

About the author: New Unionist *is the monthly newspaper published by the socialist New Union Party.*

Even though the crime rate in the United States has been declining, people's fear of crime keeps increasing.

Rising Fear of Crime

In part, this is due to profit-hungry news media sensationalizing violent crimes in a lurid race for ratings, and to fleabag politicians who run against "soft-on-crime liberals" in a squalid race for votes.

Still, fear of crime does have a basis in fact even if the crime rate is not rising. This is because violence is no longer confined to "rough" neighborhoods, but now can strike anyone, anywhere.

If people weren't plagued by other very real fears and worries over their jobs and families, they'd be able to view the crime problem more calmly and reasonably. But with all these other problems to deal with, who needs to worry that the teenager asking for spare change might one day pull a gun and demand money?

As bad as the gun-wielding muggers are, however, they are not the ones responsible for the working person's financial insecurity and all the daily complications and stress that result from not having enough money.

It is the worker's employer and elected representatives who could do something about that. But if they are unwilling to give a pay raise or to enact a national health-care plan—or are prohibited from doing so by the competitive demands of the profit system—they will certainly like to see someone else take the blame for the harm their system does to people.

So, we have the corporations' media mouthpieces and political flunkies create an image of criminal hordes terrorizing "hardworking Americans." And if these criminals can be depicted as always being from minority groups of a

From "Stop Crime: Outlaw a Criminal Economics System," editorial, *New Unionist*, August 1996. Reprinted by permission of the New Union Party, Minneapolis, Minnesota.

darker shade than white—that is, "different" from "us"—the scam will be all the more effective.

Most African Americans, Hispanic Americans and Asian Americans are themselves hardworking Americans and fear crime as much as whites. Yet, when these whole groups—as opposed to individuals within the groups—are depicted as criminally inclined, working-class blacks, whites and browns end up fearing and hating each other instead of getting together to fight the system that keeps them all on the same treadmill.

It's no mystery why inner-city minority communities are gripped by crime and violence, and the reason has nothing to do with "race."

When the steel mills shut down in Chicago and Gary, Indiana, when the auto plants were closed in Michigan, when defense and other manufacturing facilities were boarded up in south-central L.A.—when the traditional better-paying jobs open to black people started disappearing, young blacks were forced to seek economic opportunities on the streets.

Discrimination Leads to Poverty and Crime

In an earlier period of American history, Irish Americans were considered violent and criminal "by nature." At that time, the Irish were discriminated against in employment and housing and were scorned and ridiculed as ignorant, dirty and incapable of bettering themselves. Given those conditions and attitudes, the Irish *were* more likely to be arrested and wind up in court and prison.

Then it was the Italians who everyone "knew" were violent by nature. And the Poles. And the Bohemians. And every other ethnic group that occupied the bottom rung of the economic ladder at one time or another.

But once these ethnic groups were each able to improve their economic position as the economy grew and created job opportunities—which happened especially during wartime—they were accepted into the mainstream, and popular stereotypes of them as naturally violent disappeared.

With the advance of the civil-rights movement in the 1960s, it appeared that African Americans would finally be offered the same opportunity to move into the mainstream. And some progress was made, both in blacks moving into higher-level jobs, and in lessening the prejudice against them.

> *"When the traditional better-paying jobs open to black people started disappearing, young blacks were forced to seek economic opportunities on the streets."*

But then the system that had promised black people that they would have the opportunities they sought slammed the door in their face. The factory closings, job losses and wage declines of the past 20 years have affected all workers, but black workers have borne the brunt.

For the right-wing propagandists, the cause of crime is a lack of values, absent fathers and disintegrating families. These clowns present themselves as thoughtful intellectuals, but it doesn't require extraordinary insight to see that these problems are themselves the *effects*, along with crime, of economic break-down and the disappearance of jobs.

Certainly, the family is being wracked by these conditions, and children growing up without proper attention and guidance will often suffer emotionally and respond with anger and antiso-cial behavior. But sanctimonious preaching about "family values" doesn't do a thing to change the con-ditions that lead to the breakdown of the family.

> *"Lack of values, absent fathers and disintegrating families . . . are themselves the effects, along with crime, of economic breakdown and the disappearance of jobs."*

Values *are* important when it comes to shaping the behavior of young people and adults alike. The values that promote peaceful, helping, re-sponsible behavior are those which teach it is wrong to exploit or harm others for selfish gain. Cooperation, mutual aid and personal moderation are the val-ues that promote social cohesion and discourage antisocial, criminal behavior.

While these values may be paid lip service on Sunday mornings in our capi-talist society, they are not the ones that help you get ahead in this system. And getting ahead—meaning making money and acquiring property—is *the* defin-ing value of capitalism.

Capitalist Values Cause Crime

People considered "successful" in capitalist society are those who accumulate large sums of money and property. They automatically receive respect, admira-tion and deference—the very things the poorest people in society, who endure the chronic contempt or pity of society because they have no money, long most to possess.

Since the manner in which the rich got their money is secondary to the fact they have it—if it is a concern at all—there is a hazy line between fortunes ac-quired legally or illegally. In fact, nearly all of the great hereditary fortunes originated in shady dealings, outright illegality (especially bribing public offi-cials) and often violence to eliminate competitors or crush striking workers.

Of course, once "success" was achieved, the founding acquisitors and their heirs had the money to buy flattering magazine articles and biographies, to show them as "builders" and "philanthropists" rather than the thieves they re-ally were.

The big corporations of the United States are habitual lawbreakers, convicted over and over of violating anti-trust, restraint-of-trade, price-fixing, bribery, workplace health-and-safety, labor-relations and environmental-protection laws. If three-strikes-and-out were applied to their controlling executives and stock-holders, they'd all be spending the rest of their lives behind bars.

The corporations are also implicated in the crimes of the United States government, which carries on violence and terror the world over. It is their property and profits that are being protected when the U.S. military smashes attempts by other countries to control their own oil and other natural wealth, or when the CIA directs its puppet dictators to murder workers and peasants fighting the exploitation of the multinationals.

Drugs are often cited as a major factor in violent crime.

The reason the drug business is so violent is that it's so profitable. When free enterprise operates outside the legal boundaries that try to keep business competition nonviolent, any and all methods to get ahead of the competition are acceptable and used. The quickest and most effective method is, of course, mayhem and murder.

> *"The capitalist system itself is based on theft."*

An illegal business of such size and scope as the drug business could not continue without regular and sizeable payoffs to cops, prosecutors, judges, politicians and officeholders. Panama is a major conduit of the South to North America drug flow. Not coincidentally, most of the world's major banks are located there to take part in the resulting cash flow. The drug trade is part and parcel of the "legitimate" profit economy and political system, and the smart money understands that the so-called "war on drugs" is nothing but a public-relations scam.

The Capitalist System Is Criminal

Crime and the acquisitive values of capitalism are also inseparable. The people on the top cheat, lie and kill—or pay others to cheat, lie and kill—to get what they want. They are the ones who establish the moral standards for the rest of society. The muggers on the street are merely imitating their example to get what they want.

The capitalist system itself is based on theft. All the goods and services labor produces are stolen by a small group of capitalist owners. What the workers get out of the deal is a wage to keep them alive and in good working order.

But more often than not, the system can't even provide that much to its workers, or enough jobs for all who need one. That's when people are pushed to more extreme measures—to crime—to get money. As more and more people get left behind in the "global economy," society will inevitably get more violent, regardless how many cops are on the street or how many prisons are built.

Does this mean we just have to accept a future of rising poverty, crime and violence?

No! In fact, there is no rational reason for these conditions continuing because more than enough wealth and productive capacity already exist to meet the material needs of all. The main problem, from which all other social problems flow, is that private profit, not human need, is the goal of economic activity today.

Instead of mindlessly shooting at each other, the 80% of the population getting ripped off by the 1% should be directing their fire at the top. Not with guns, but with self-education, economic organization and political action, all directed toward taking back the wealth of the nation for the people.

This is the only long-run solution to crime. It is also the only effective short-run strategy because it alone offers a way for alienated and angry young people to return to the working-class community and be accepted on a basis of equality! It shows them how to direct their anger productively against the system, instead of self-destructively against their neighbors.

Social Decay Invites Crime

by George L. Kelling and Catherine M. Coles

About the authors: *George L. Kelling and Catherine M. Coles are the authors of* Fixing "Broken Windows": Restoring Order in American Cities.

In the current debate over what to do about crime in America, national political leaders focus on the "grand" crime issues—capital punishment, gun control, the length of prison sentences, and the number of police on the streets. But on the local level, the terms of debate are much different. There, the issues may seem relatively trivial: panhandling, lying down in public spaces, public drinking and drug use, prostitution, unsolicited window washing, public urination and defecation, loitering, and graffiti. Yet the skirmishes being fought over these issues in areas such as Boston's Dorchester, San Francisco's Tenderloin area, Milwaukee's Near West Side, Seattle's Wallingford area, and New York City's Columbia Heights may well determine whether or not these areas continue to decay.

The Homeless and the Crime Problem

What is going on? Why do local debates appear to center on problems so different from those focused upon in current national crime legislation? Isn't "serious" crime the real problem? Is it true, as Helen Hershkoff of the American Civil Liberties Union (ACLU) argues, that: "In an effort to deal with the enormous increase in poverty and homelessness in cities across the country during the past decade, numerous municipalities are enforcing, with renewed vigor, long-dormant ordinances prohibiting the destitute from asking members of the public for money"?

Are we resurrecting Victorian ideas of the "dangerous classes" and returning to the bad old days of arresting people for the "offenses" of poverty and homelessness?

No, we think not. The local issues are far more complex than such formulations would suggest. On the one hand, academics and civil libertarians properly worry about issues such as freedom of speech and due process. On the other, residents in many urban neighborhoods see controlling disorder as a last-ditch

From George L. Kelling and Catherine M. Coles, "Disorder and the Court." Reprinted with permission of the authors and the *Public Interest*, no. 116, Summer 1994, pp. 57-75; ©1994 by National Affairs, Inc.

effort to restore safety and civility to streets, parks, and other public spaces. Crime statistics may rise or fall; citizens' daily "in your face" street experiences tell them that things are out of control and worsening.

The Law

Things have not always been as they are now. For most of American history, in nearly every state and in many municipalities, there were laws against begging, indigence, and traveling about the country without visible means of support.

Following the Depression and World War II, criticism of vagrancy and loitering laws became increasingly common. In 1972, in *Papachristou v. City of Jacksonville*, the Supreme Court struck down an anti-vagrancy statute. Then, in 1983, in *Kolender v. Lawson*, the Supreme Court struck down a California statute which required that loiterers produce identification and account for their presence on the request of a police officer.

Following the Supreme Court's decisions in *Papachristou* and *Kolender*, other courts overturned many vagrancy and loitering laws under the due process clause of the Fourteenth Amendment. States and municipalities got the message, and as a result police ceased to enforce, and district attorneys to prosecute under, those anti-begging and panhandling laws that remained on the books.

Other localities took a different path, and passed more specific, behavior-directed statutes and ordinances. Both a 1965 Supreme Court decision, *Shuttlesworth v. City of Birmingham*, and a series of New York cases beginning in the late 1960s set forth the rule that while legislation prohibiting loitering alone was unconstitutional, legislation prohibiting "loitering for the purpose of" committing some specific unlawful act, such as prostitution, was acceptable.

In recent challenges to loitering laws, however, the courts have been presented not only with Fourteenth Amendment due process and equal protection arguments, but with assertions that such laws infringe upon the First Amendment right to free speech. In some cases the courts have found First Amendment concerns sufficiently compelling to overturn even "loitering for the purpose of" laws, signalling a further shift in legal thinking. Legislators have responded by

> *"Crime statistics may rise or fall; citizens' daily 'in your face' street experiences tell them that things are out of control and worsening."*

developing laws against very specific behaviors—lying down, asking a person for money more than once, not allowing people to move freely on sidewalks, etc. But even this strategy may not succeed if the courts continue to hold that the First Amendment rights of street people outweigh the countervailing interests of a community. It is this most recent judicial shift that is the concern of this viewpoint.

In a word, we believe that many of these decisions have gone too far, interfering with a community's ability to maintain order on its streets, in its parks, and in other public places. Furthermore, we believe that the resulting disorder has had serious social consequences—increasing fear and crime, and driving out law-abiding citizens.

But we believe that the root problem here is a social, and not just a legal, one. That is, in reaching their decisions, the courts have relied on current, popular assumptions about disorderly behavior—the assumptions accepted and promoted by the media, policy makers, and advocates. But, as a growing body of evidence indicates, the assumptions are incorrect. Refuting them must be the first step if we are to change the direction of recent court decisions.

The Problem

During the late 1980s and early 1990s, one of the authors of this viewpoint worked with New York City's Transit Authority Police Department to study the problems posed by the relatively small group of persons who used the subway to panhandle, "hang out," urinate and defecate, sleep, and consume drugs and alcohol. Passengers were increasingly fearful of this be-

> *"Many [court] decisions have gone too far, interfering with a community's ability to maintain order on its streets."*

havior, and surveys revealed that this was contributing to a decline in subway ridership: 97 percent of passengers reported taking some form of defensive action before entering the subway, 75 percent refrained from wearing expensive clothing or jewelry, 69 percent avoided "certain people," 68 percent avoided particular platform locations, and 61 percent avoided specific train cars.

Many social advocates and a good portion of the media argued that the problem in the subways was "homelessness," created by a lack of adequate housing and employment. These social advocates and the media were suspicious of relying on the police to address the problem, since the police, in their view, just wanted to "throw the bums out," regardless of the consequences. The advocates believed that those who did not want to allow the homeless to use the subway for shelter were the "well-to-do," who were disregarding the needs and interests of the poor. These assumptions were shared by much of the staff of the Metropolitan Transportation Authority (MTA) and the New York City Transit Authority. Repeated attempts were made to refer this population to agencies, give them food, transport them to shelters (provided by the Volunteers of America with MTA funding), and to bring social workers into the subway. These efforts, however, were for naught. As the number of people attempting to use the subway as a surrogate shelter continued to increase, pressure mounted on the subway's Transit Police Department (TPD) to do something.

The Real Homeless Problem

The author's analysis—which consisted of observations, public surveys, and a literature review—suggested that popular conceptions were off the mark. Those who used the subway for shelter were a particularly troubled distillate of drug and alcohol abusers, the mentally ill, and criminals. MTA estimates indicated that at least 40 percent of the subway homeless were mentally ill. Substantial portions of the remainder were chronic alcohol and drug abusers. Some were genuinely homeless, but not because they were temporarily out of work or because there was a shortage of homes, as portrayed in the media. To the contrary, many were extraordinarily disturbed and in need of medical and social services. Many others lived off their criminal activities, which included preying on passengers.

> *"The problem in the subway, then, was not homelessness per se; the problem was rule-violating behavior."*

The problem in the subway, then, was not homelessness per se; the problem was rule-violating behavior by an extraordinarily troubled group, mostly male, and in large part minority. This finding has been replicated in broader contexts: in New York City, 80 percent of the males in armory shelters abuse drugs or alcohol. In *A Nation in Denial: The Truth About Homelessness*, Alice S. Baum and Donald W. Burnes, both of whom worked with the homeless in social service roles, found that the popular portrayal of the "homeless problem" was way off the mark:

> [N]ewspapers, magazines, books, and television programs reported stories of homeless two-parent rust-belt families temporarily down on their luck or of homeless individuals who had recently been laid off from permanent employment. These stories led policymakers, politicians, and advocates to frame the issue as one of people not having homes and therefore being "homeless." None of these descriptions bore any resemblance to the people we knew. Nor were they consistent with the emerging research, which documented that up to 85 percent of all homeless adults suffer from chronic alcoholism, drug addictions, mental illness, or some combination of the three, often complicated by serious mental problems.

In sum, the terms of the local debate have largely been framed by advocates of a particular, and scarcely disguised, political agenda—an agenda concerned with social injustice, society's inequitable distribution of wealth, and the general victimization of helpless street people. We have no quarrel with this political agenda per se, or attempts to implement it, even through the courts. Moreover, we believe that the concerns raised by homeless advocates are very much worthy of debate. Nevertheless, an alternative perspective exists, and is supported by a substantial factual base. To the extent that courts ignore this perspective, and the facts that support it, and adhere to the usual ideas about the homeless, they are either inadvertently or wantonly supporting a political agenda and obfuscating the complex psychological, social, and economic problems that have led to our current urban crisis.

There are serious consequences of misunderstanding our troublesome street population: first, the very real emotional and social disabilities of this population are not recognized, let alone adequately addressed. Second, the enormous social consequences of this group's behavior—that is, the effects on other people—are not recognized. In the remainder of this viewpoint, we focus on the second of these consequences.

In many recent decisions, courts have tended either not to understand the enormous social consequences of fear and disorder, or to ignore them. Indeed, many have trivialized the problem, as did Judge Robert W. Sweet in *Loper v. New York City Police Dept.*:

> A peaceful beggar poses no threat to society. The beggar has arguably only committed the offense of being needy. The message one or one hundred beggars sends society can be disturbing. If some portion of society is offended, the answer is not in criminalizing these people, debtor's prisons being long gone, but addressing the root cause of their existence. . . . Professor Kelling's approach would simply remove the messenger of bad news. . . .

Judge Sweet suggests that society is offended by the notion of neediness. Perhaps, partially. But more importantly, individual citizens, of all social classes, are *threatened* by the behavior of, and the implicit and explicit threats made by, serious substance abusers, emotionally disturbed persons, some "peaceful beggars," and criminals. Not just panhandling, but prostitution, public urination and defecation, drunkenness, and obstreperousness all send a chilling message to citizens. This message is: things are out of control. For most citizens, disorder *is* the crime problem.

Disorder and Fear

Social science research confirms the link between disorder and fear. This link was demonstrated as early as 1967, when Albert Biderman and his associates found the connection in a survey of citizens in Washington, D.C. Likewise Nathan Glazer, in "On Subway Graffiti in New York City" in the Winter 1979 *Public Interest*, suggested that ubiquitous graffiti on subway cars signalled riders that public officials did not have control. And if public

"There are serious consequences of misunderstanding our troublesome street population."

officials could not control relatively minor problems such as graffiti, they certainly could not control serious problems such as robbery and assault. Graffiti and robbery were of one ilk to citizens.

The link between disorder and fear was brought to mainstream attention in 1982 when James Q. Wilson and George L. Kelling published "Broken Windows" in the *Atlantic Monthly*. The article identified various violations of community norms that, while often codified as illegal, at times were not: public drinking, panhandling, prostitution, loud music, and graffiti.

The article discussed the link between disorder and community fear. Also, it argued that just as an unrepaired broken window sends a message that no one cares and invites more damage, so unattended disorderly behavior also acts as a signal that no one cares, with the result of more disorderly behavior and serious crime. Finally "Broken Windows" argued that disorder left unattended leads to a breakdown of community controls, and ultimately undermines the fabric of urban life and social intercourse. But much of this article's thesis was new and untested. Unlike the link between disorder and fear, which had been explored in previous research, the relationship between disorder and crime, and between disorder and further urban decay, had not.

Disorder and Serious Crime

In his 1990 book *Disorder and Decline*, Wesley Skogan confirmed the correlation between disorder and serious crime. Using survey and observational data collected in forty residential neighborhoods in six U.S. cities, Skogan found that: (1) broad consensus existed among members of all racial and ethnic groups as to what constituted disorderly behavior; (2) disorder was a precursor to serious crime; and (3) disorder was also a precursor to further urban decay.

"For most citizens, disorder is the crime problem."

By "precursor" to crime and urban decay, Skogan meant that disorder was found in the study to be one of several variables sequentially linked to crime and urban decay. There were other explanatory factors—such as poverty and family instability—but disorder was the single most powerful precursor of both serious crime and urban decay.

Skogan's findings clearly suggest that controlling disorderly behavior is important both because it will reduce fear (which will make people more comfortable in city streets, parks, and public transportation systems) and because it will discourage violent crime and help prevent urban decay. Contemporary experience confirms these findings. Focus groups in New Haven, Connecticut, surveys in the Fenway area of Boston, and interviews with suburbanites near San Francisco and with merchants in Brooklyn all show the same result: disorder creates fear. In response to this fear, citizens have abandoned parks and public spaces, refrained from using public transportation, turned from neighborhood shopping areas to malls, hired private security, locked themselves behind doors and barred their windows, purchased dogs and guns, and in some cases deserted cities entirely.

In other words, these findings show that it is crucially important for order to be maintained. When it is not, the social consequences can be severe.

Genetic Factors May Cause Criminal Behavior

by Chi Chi Sileo

About the author: *Chi Chi Sileo is a former contributing editor of* Insight, *a weekly newsmagazine.*

In the movie *The Bad Seed*, a mother reluctantly comes to realize that her angelic-looking little girl is a cold-blooded killer. That was fiction, of course—a story that built on the notion that someone could be "born bad"—and was overly simplistic as an explanation of evil. But new research is suggesting that that notion might be closer to truth than previously believed.

Scientists have begun to ask whether there is something biologically "wrong," or different, about people who become violent criminals. And they are disclosing intriguing answers. Moreover, they say, criminal behavior can be spotted at a very early age—even as young as 6 years old, the age of the girl in the movie.

Traditional Theories: Society Causes Crime

Theories about the causes of violent crime go all over the intellectual map, drawing from sociology, psychology, philosophy and religion. The question bedevils law enforcement workers, prison counselors, the criminal justice system and an increasingly frightened public. Is crime rooted in poverty, poor upbringing, exposure to "the underclass" or lack of exposure to moral teachings? Is evil, pure and simple, the "bad seed" come to life? And more disturbingly, is violence an innate drive, something held at bay by a fragile line separating most of us, perhaps only temporarily, from a violent few?

"It isn't all that hard to understand why some people use violence," says Robert Hare, a professor of psychology at the University of British Columbia and author of *Without Conscience: The Disturbing World of the Psychopaths Among Us*. "It's much more difficult to understand why we're so well-socialized not to."

According to Hare, most violent criminals, particularly "cold-blooded" psychopaths, are just living examples of natural human behavior carried to a logical extreme. "Criminals have not acquired the norms of society," he says. "To them, criminal behavior just makes sense. They haven't made a conscious choice to be bad, they're just doing what comes naturally and what most benefits them. They are doing what we all would do if we didn't have social controls."

In 1986, an international group of social scientists and biologists meeting in Spain issued the historic Seville Statement on Violence, which emphatically declared that aggression is not an innate human drive. Heralded as an optimistic statement about humanity, especially for its implication that war is not a necessary evil, the Seville Statement also helped to give scientific authority to the society-as-cause theories that have held sway in studies of crime for the past few decades. These theories indict society itself for peoples' violent choices and pin the blame on everything from unemployment and poor schools to television violence and rap-music lyrics.

> *"Scientists have begun to ask whether there is something biologically 'wrong,' or different, about people who become violent criminals."*

"The conventional thinking is alive and well," states Stanton Samenow, an Alexandria, Virginia, psychologist who works closely with different prison systems and has authored numerous books on crime. "It seems people are ready to blame everything but the federal deficit for crime—and that may be next."

Genetic Theories of Violence

Maybe not. A brave new field of genetic research is debunking those theories and unearthing evidence that the propensity for violence is, in fact, an elemental human trait—one of which some people just happen to have more.

"Of course this is all very 'un-PC.' But to say that all criminals are made and not born is nonsensical," says Hare. "People are born with all kinds of different propensities: fear, timidity, cheerfulness, as well as different physical traits. Why should it be any different for this particular trait?"

"Violence is a normal human predisposition that exists to a higher degree in people who eventually become criminals," asserts psychologist Adrian Raine, whose groundbreaking studies are among the first to confirm what many criminologists long have suspected. Raine, an associate professor at the University of Southern California, recently completed a series of studies that show differences in genetic composition and brain functioning between criminals and noncriminals.

In one study, Raine used brain imaging to explore differences in the brains of violent offenders. Using a technique called positron emission tomography—which measures amounts of glucose metabolism produced when the brain is working—Raine found that violent offenders showed a marked dysfunction in the specific region of the brain that controls aggression.

"We know that violent offenders are impulsive, often don't think ahead," Raine notes, "and now we have a better understanding of why."

Crime Provides Stimulation to Criminals

In another study, Raine found that criminals have very low natural levels of physiological arousal measured by elements such as skin conductance (sweat), heart rate and electrical activity in the brain. Since low levels of arousal are uncomfortable, these people often look for external ways to get themselves "fired up." Some will look for stimulation in sex, drugs, fast driving and high-risk sports such as bungee jumping, for example; some will turn to crime.

"Crime is an arousal jag," Raine explains. "It's very interesting; we found that when we interviewed burglars, for instance, the word that kept coming up was 'exciting'—breaking into houses was a real thrill for them."

That jibes with the experiences recounted by Jeffrey Smalldon, a forensic psychologist in Columbus, Ohio, who has worked with violent criminals. "We talk about crimes being 'motiveless' or 'senseless,'" he says, "but it just means that their motives are motives that don't make sense to us. What they net is not necessarily money, it's something more subtle and obscure. It's in the process, the predation, the cunning, the pulling it off. That's the high."

Raine's study looked at schoolchildren as well, since most indicators of criminal activity show up at very early ages. Many of these students had been branded "antisocial" by their teachers; however, even among that group of kids, the ones with naturally high arousal levels did not engage in criminal or violent behavior. "The protective factor here is high levels of arousal," Raine reported. Some of the teenagers had natural levels of arousal that were higher than those of normal, or not antisocial, teens, and that seemed to be the factor that kept them in line.

The real importance of Raine's studies is in the possibility of using this knowledge to nip crime in the bud. For example, Raine has been training people in biofeedback, an easy-to-learn technique that allows people to track and raise their arousal levels. Biofeedback is used medically with people who suffer from hypertension and can succeed in raising arousal levels in as few as 21 sessions. According to Raine, combining biofeedback training with educational programs would provide the best way to prevent at-risk adolescents from getting into trouble.

"The propensity for violence is, in fact, an elemental human trait—one of which some people just happen to have more."

The study on brain imaging also has led to significant possibilities for intervention. Cognitive remediation, a type of therapy used to help stroke victims, the head-injured and others who have lost or damaged certain brain parts or functions, trains parts of the brain to take over the jobs performed by lost or weakened parts. Murderers have a marked lack of functioning, measured by glucose, in a very specific region of the brain, the region that controls aggressive behavior. Raine believes that cognitive remediation could be used to train other brain regions to take over those functions but adds that the research "is speculative at this point."

Environment Plays a Part

Still, he and other researchers are quick to point out that "biology is not destiny." These genetic studies indicate only a predisposition to violence, not a predestination to it. To become a violent criminal, they say, the genetic predisposition must be fostered by the right environment: This comes down to the family.

Parental neglect, especially maternal neglect, is a key factor in destroying the ability to form attachments. And attachments—to family, to community, to outside goals—are what keep most people from becoming criminals. Maternal neglect, whether by accident or the mother's choice, includes physical or emotional abuse, improper nutrition and even premature birth—anything that upsets the natural bonding process.

Physical abuse or harsh treatment are the primary factors that can confirm a predisposition to violence. "Aggression and harsh treatment at home works in two ways," says Ervin Staub, author of *The Roots of Evil*, a study of genocide. "First, it makes the child less trusting, more hostile. Secondly, it demonstrates that aggression is a tool, and you need skills to use a tool. So the child learns very well how to use violence. This isn't true in all cases, but enough to point to a definite trend." That conclusion is echoed by virtually every researcher in the field.

Most of these experts also note that the most common kind of violence children face is agonizingly close to home: corporal punishment. According to Philip Greven, author of *Spare the Child: The Religious Roots of Punishment and the Psychological Impact of Physical Abuse*, many studies show that children who are physically disciplined are far more likely to become criminals and use violence against others.

"Both aggression and altruism are cases of 'learning by doing,'" says Staub. "Children model the behavior they see and experience. If they are treated in a positive way, that's how they'll treat others. If they're treated harshly, that's how they'll behave."

That explanation, however, isn't universally observed.

"My theory is that it isn't the environment that determines how people behave," counters Samenow, "it's how people choose to respond to that environment." Samenow, who scorns what he calls a blame-the-parents mentality, points out that often what appears to be harsh and neglectful behavior by parents is actually a perfectly understandable response to children who have parents at their wits' end.

> *"To become a violent criminal, . . . the genetic predisposition must be fostered by the right environment: This comes down to the family."*

"Of course, environment can affect behavior," Samenow writes in his book *Before It's Too Late: Why Some Kids Get into Trouble and What Parents Can Do About It*, "but the longer I have been involved in research and practice the more I have been compelled to recognize an even more important fact: The environment from which a person comes is less crucial than the choice the individual makes as he responds to that environment."

> *"The environment from which a person comes is less crucial than the choice the individual makes as he responds to that environment."*

Samenow, like Staub, is not convinced that there are genetic bases for violent behavior, but he argues that it doesn't matter anyway; criminals, he says, simply think differently than non-criminals do. They see the world and their place in it in ways almost unrecognizable to the rest of us. "That's true across crimes. And even if they made certain things legal, say drugs, some one with that pattern of thinking would just find another law to break." Samenow believes that crime can be prevented by a two-part plan: stepping in early, when patterns of antisocial behavior start cropping up, and using the kind of tough-minded, confrontational "therapy" he uses in prisons.

Opposition to Genetic Research

Samenow does not actively oppose genetic research; but there are those who do. The field is ripe for controversy, and not just in theory: The 1992 appointment of Frederick Goodwin to be director of the National Institute of Mental Health almost was derailed because of Goodwin's work in genetic bases of violent behavior which was called racist because it discussed violence among inner-city minorities. A conference that Goodwin had planned on violence in the inner cities was canceled.

"The real irony is that it's the inner cities who are being most hurt by violent crime," Raine notes, although he acknowledges that this type of research must be performed with a constant vigilance against abuse.

"When you talk about predispositions to undesirable behavior, you get into fears of genetic engineering, eugenics, genocide—everything associated with Nazism," says Raine. He understands allegations of racism but points out that every one of these studies has used whites as subjects precisely to avoid any taint of racial bias.

Ideological battles also are at stake. A majority of sociologists and criminologists still believe in society-is-all theories, and government crime-prevention programs reflect those beliefs. Raine predicts that by providing early care to at-risk mothers to reduce birth complications and maternal rejection, violent crime could be reduced by up to 22 percent. He acknowledges the ethical dilemma of targeting certain people for intervention but argues that this kind of specific intervention would be far more effective than current one-size-fits-all programs that address crime after it occurs rather than preventing it from happening.

The Criminally Predisposed Can Change Their Ways

"No one wants to hear this," says Smalldon, "but we can predict violent tendencies at a very early age. And that's when we should be stepping in, before these children go right over the edge. Of course, this is very controversial and highly charged, like we're saying that the 'bad seed' is a fact. But it isn't like that. The little girl in *The Bad Seed* was out-and-out evil; we know that we can intervene and people really can change their ways."

> *"It's the lethal combination of a violent predisposition and childhood disruption that appear as constants among violent offenders."*

Raine, Hare and other researchers stress that criminal behavior is not purely a result of genetic makeup; rather, it's the lethal combination of a violent predisposition and childhood disruption that appear as constants among violent offenders.

The hope these researchers share is that ideological and political controversies won't put a stop to their work. They point out that far from expressing a "you're doomed" philosophy, these findings point to a future filled with hope. "We can change biology," Raine says. "We can change violence and crime." Rather than rail at these new studies, he notes, people should embrace the opportunity to replace the failed theories of the past with new and different ones that might just offer a better way out.

"When we close the door on biological research," he says, "we open the doors to a far greater tragedy."

A Lack of Morals Causes Criminal Behavior

by Robert James Bidinotto

About the author: *Robert James Bidinotto is a staff writer for* Reader's Digest *and the editor of the book* Criminal Justice? The Legal System Versus Individual Responsibility.

Since 1960, per capita crime rates have more than tripled, while violent crime rates have nearly quintupled. By any measure, we live in a nation much less safe than that in which our parents grew up.

Liberal and Conservative Explanations of Crime

This simply cries out for an explanation. What in our modern society could possibly account for the sudden and explosive growth in force, fraud, and coercion?

Liberals typically posit socio-economic factors, such as poverty. Yet how can we attribute the rising tide of violence to rising poverty, when the periods of fastest crime growth have been during times of rapidly rising American wealth?

This popular "explanation" also fails on comparative grounds. Why is the richest nation on earth experiencing increases in predatory behavior that vastly exceed crime rates in much poorer nations? Why now, at a time of relative abundance and wealth, instead of during impoverished times past—say, during our Great Depression? And why after decades of dumping trillions of dollars into programs to eradicate privation, hunger, illiteracy, insecurity, disease, homelessness—the alleged "root causes" of crime?

Liberal explanations for crime that blame psychological or biological factors also fall flat. Why, for example, would there have been an abrupt leap in mental illness or genetic defects starting in 1962, when crime rates began to take off?

However, I must also challenge a common conservative explanation for rising crime: blaming it on the welfare state.

Though a governmental "safety net" of sorts has existed since the New Deal, the modern American welfare state wasn't enacted into law until the Great So-

From Robert James Bidinotto, "The 'Root Causes' of Crime," *Freeman,* June 1995. Reprinted by permission of the *Freeman;* ©1995 by the Foundation for Economic Education.

ciety, and didn't begin to make its impact felt until the end of the 1960s. Yet crime rates began to soar *before* that—in the *early* 1960s. How can we attribute rising crime to a welfare state which didn't then exist?

Second, criminal behavior patterns start in youth, peaking in the late teen years. Whatever caused crime to explode in the 1960s would have had to been planted in young people during their formative years: in the 1950s. Where was the 1950s welfare state?

> *"Liberal and conservative explanations for criminality share a common root: they blame factors outside the criminal himself."*

Third, many nations have had welfare states far longer than America, yet have crime rates far lower than ours. Why?

Finally, U.S. crime rates have begun in recent years to level out, even decline a bit. Has there been any corresponding decline in welfare statism to "cause" this? Clearly not.

These liberal and conservative explanations for criminality share a common root: they blame factors *outside* the criminal himself. Liberals say "poverty made him do it." Conservatives say "welfare checks made him do it." Both share the false premise of economic determinism.

The Causes of Law-Abiding Behavior

It is more fruitful to ask not "What causes crime?" but "What causes us *not* to commit crimes?" Social scientists posit two reasons: what they refer to as "external and internal constraints on behavior."

External constraints are deterrents. We don't commit crimes for fear of negative consequences, or punishments. Internal constraints, by contrast, are what we used to call "conscience." Most people accept certain moral standards; and when we violate those standards, we feel guilty about it. Our guilt feelings inhibit us from committing crimes—even when we think we can get away with them.

My view is that crime has increased because of a systematic erosion in recent decades of *both* external *and* internal constraints on behavior. Deterrence has been weakened, while conscience has been deadened.

Consider, first, the undermining of deterrence. For half a century, utilitarian prescriptions for crime control amounted to giving endless "second chances" to juvenile criminals, repeated probationary sentences to adult felons, and speedy releases to the relative few who landed behind bars.

In 1949 the U.S. Supreme Court declared that retribution was "no longer the dominant objective of the criminal law," but should be replaced by "reformation and rehabilitation." Former Attorney General Ramsey Clark, in his influential 1970 book, *Crime in America*, declared that "Punishment as an end in itself is itself a crime in our times. . . . Rehabilitation must be the goal of modern corrections. Every other consideration should be subordinated to it."

And so it was. The odds of punishment for a given crime have fallen sharply over the past 30 years. Today, a person who commits a serious crime has a better than 98 percent chance of avoiding prison. And thanks to early parole and generous "good time" allowances, the typical inmate serves only a third of his court-imposed sentence.

The Erosion of Moral Codes

The undermining of external constraints is only a part of the problem. More important is the erosion of internal constraints.

Most of us go about our daily business with a secure sense of routine. We walk past co-workers, sit with family members, wait in grocery store lines, seldom giving a thought to our personal safety. But imagine what it would be like to live in a world in which all these people suddenly, inexplicably, violently turned on you. In such a jungle, human life would become impossible. We would live like animals; our operative premise would no longer be "live and let live," but "kill or be killed."

We have not yet reached that stage, but the signs of social deterioration are unmistakable. More and more people act like speeding vehicles without steering wheels or brakes, leaving in their wake a growing trail of bloodshed and destruction.

A moral code is the source of "internal constraints on behavior." It is the rudder of any culture, which keeps it from crashing against the shoals of violence, and sinking into chaos. Yet modern intellectuals, wedded to relativism, have not only abandoned the helm of moral leadership: they assault anyone who dares to assume it. Their normative vandalism has been so complete that today, even to use words such as "morality," "conscience," or "virtue," invites mockery and the rolling of eyes.

> *"Crime has increased because of a systematic erosion in recent decades of* **both** *external* **and** *internal constraints on behavior."*

These intellectuals have virtually obliterated all external and internal constraints. As utilitarians, they have undermined deterrence. As relativists, they have eliminated guilt. They have thus unleashed the sociopaths we see around us—savages who act with impunity, and without conscience.

We rightfully expect our justice system to impose external constraints on those lacking internal constraints. But we can never hire enough police, or build enough prisons, if our underlying *moral* crisis is not addressed. The real roots of criminality lie in the moral abdication occurring in our homes, communities, and institutions.

Restoring moral direction is not a job we dare delegate to politicians. Rather, if our culture is to survive, we ourselves must begin to uphold, fight for, and inculcate the values and standards upon which any civilization rests.

A Lack of Religion Does Not Cause Crime

by Lisa Conyers and Philip D. Harvey

About the authors: *Lisa Conyers is a writer and researcher in Mount Vernon, Washington. Philip D. Harvey is a public policy researcher and writer in Washington, D.C.*

Charles W. Colson, the convicted Watergate felon, went on after prison to found a volunteer program for reforming prisoners [Prison Fellowship]. As part of that program, he advocated the broader use of religious values to help break "America's seemingly indomitable cycle of crime."

Religion and Crime

In a talk before the National Press Club in Washington, D.C., Colson chided the media for giving "short shrift" to religious values, "including the acknowledgment of the relevance of morality in society."

But how relevant is religion to morality? Does religion make a person more ethical? Can a strong dose of religion really reduce crime?

Surprisingly, recent research suggests that a religious person is more likely to commit a crime than a non-religious person. One can even argue that the more religious the society, the more likely it is to have high crime rates.

What's more, studies indicate that a believer in a religion is less likely to do a good deed than is a non-believer. Religion alone, many researchers agree, does not determine personal moral behavior.

Renowned sociologist Alfie Kohn, author of *No Contest: The Case Against Competition* and *You Know What They Say . . . The Truth About Popular Beliefs*, has taken on the myths surrounding altruism and empathy in his recent book, *The Brighter Side of Human Nature*. With this book he continues his reasoned refutation of popular beliefs, proving that man is by nature as likely to be altruistic as selfish or gentle as opposed to aggressive. This book reviews the available research on the impact of religion on behavior and brings us Kohn's conclusion that "religious faith appears to be neither necessary for one to act

From Lisa Conyers and Philip D. Harvey, "Religion and Crime: Do They Go Together?" *Free Inquiry,* Summer 1996. Reprinted by permission of *Free Inquiry.*

pro-socially nor sufficient to ensure such behavior."

Kohn adds there is "virtually no connection one way or the other" between religious belief or affiliation and pro-social activities.

Among studies Kohn cites is one done on 700 city dwellers. It found that religious people were no more likely to be sociable, helpful to neighbors, or eager to participate in neighborhood groups than non-religious people.

In another study, researchers asked students about their religious affiliation and their willingness to cheat on a test. The majority of only one group resisted cheating: atheists.

Religion Does Not Promote Good Deeds

Kohn also describes an experiment in which researchers told students that a person in another room had just fallen off a ladder. The finding: There was no relationship between a student's belief in the Bible's accuracy and his or her willingness to aid the ladder "victim."

Two thousand years of preachments about the Good Samaritan have not changed an "obvious fact about altruism," explains Morton Hunt, another avid researcher into human nature. People tend to practice altruism toward those in their own group, Hunt says, but not those outside it, "for whom they feel anything from indifference to hatred."

Hunt is the author of seventeen books in the behavioral and social sciences, including the best-selling *The Universe Within* and *Profiles of Social Research: The Scientific Study of Human Interactions*. He is a frequent contributor to the *New York Times* magazine and is well known as a behavioral scientist. In his book Hunt cites extensive research done by Samuel and Pearl Oliner on rescuers of Jews during World War II. Their analysis shows that 90% of the rescuers had had religious upbringing, yet only 15% cited religion

> *"Recent research suggests that a religious person is more likely to commit a crime than a non-religious person."*

as the main reason for what they did. Further, there was no significant difference between the religiosity of rescuers and that of a control group.

In his book *The Compassionate Beast: What Science Is Discovering About the Humane Side of Humankind*, Hunt writes: "It has not only been Goths, Huns and other barbarians who have relished slaughtering their enemies; civilized people, whose religions exalt altruism and the love of mankind, have done likewise."

Logician-philosopher Bertrand Russell went even further in *Why I Am Not a Christian*:

> The more intense has been the religion of any period and the more profound has been the dogmatic belief, the greater has been the cruelty and the worse has been the state of affairs. . . .

> You find as you look around the world that every single bit of progress in humane feeling, every improvement in criminal law, every step towards the

diminution of war, every step towards better treatment of the colored races, every moral progress that there has been in the world, has been consistently opposed by the organized churches of the world.

Does Religion Deter Crime?

If religion does not deter war, can it at least deter crime? Is there any evidence that Charles Colson's project to instill more religion in prisoners will cut the rate of violence? Not according to research by Lee Ellis of the University of North Dakota at Minot. Dr. Ellis has published widely in the social sciences on the topics of religiosity, criminal and violent behavior, rape and sexual behavior. He has devoted a lifetime to examining the relationship between religion and crime.

> *"Man is by nature as likely to be altruistic as selfish or gentle as opposed to aggressive."*

In comparing denominational religions, Ellis found Jews to be the least criminal, by far, and Catholics the most. But a group showing a crime rate equal to or lower than that of Jews was one composed of people claiming no religious affiliation. Seeking further empirical confirmation, Ellis is conducting a study of 16,000 respondents to see if he can replicate those findings. Ellis is also conducting a comparison of crime rates with available information on religious affiliation by country, to see if he can further support his findings.

Sociologists William Sims Bainbridge and Rodney Stark of Towson State University in Maryland differ with Ellis over the part religion plays in impeding crime. They argue that religion itself does not decide whether a person will commit a crime. What is crucial, they say, is whether the group or society to which that individual belongs is religious and enforces religious values. Any strong social group that molds behavior, even a high school sports team, can determine whether a person will behave morally.

Bainbridge and Stark support their views with analyses of large computer databases. Their grist includes crime statistics from the Department of Justice for every county in the country. It also contains data on religious groups gathered by the Census Bureau and services for the study of religion.

In a brief demonstration of their database, Bainbridge showed a strong correlation between areas of low church membership and larceny. He then wiped out that correlation by introducing a second variable, transience. He found that transience relates strongly, too, to many other crimes.

Bainbridge says: "Even if you do not consider yourself a religious person, you are only a generation or two removed from a religious upbringing, and you also live in a society in which the majority are religious, and religious values are ingrained in the laws and social rules of the society. Therefore, you are in fact influenced by religion and that religion instills values in you. The United States is in fact a very religious country."

Evidence from other sources supports Bainbridge's last sentence. Statistics from *Where We Stand*, a book written by the World Rank Research Team, suggests that 91% of the population in the United States believes in God. That compares with 48% in the United Kingdom and 47% in Japan.

The percent of people who believe in their religious leaders is 43% in the United States. It is only 6% in Japan and 3% in the United Kingdom

> *"If religious communities thwart crime, one would expect to find a very low crime rate in the United States."*

and Germany. The portion believing in hell is 76% in the United States. Compare that with 53% in Japan, 38% in Australia, 35% in the United Kingdom, and 16% in Germany.

The Gallup Poll finds that 81% of people in the United States consider themselves religious persons. That is two points lower than Italy, but well ahead of Ireland, Spain, Great Britain, West Germany, Hungary, France, and Scandinavia. Ireland far surpasses the United States in the number of people who attend church at least weekly. Still, the United States leads most other major countries by a wide margin.

Those figures, Ellis counters, simply prove the fallacy of Bainbridge's argument. If America is very religious, and if religious communities thwart crime, one would expect to find a very low crime rate in the United States. The opposite is true; the United States is among the most criminal, violent countries in the industrialized world.

Where We Stand cites these figures: The United States has 8.4 murders per 100,000 people. Rates in Germany, Australia, Portugal, France, Denmark, and Canada range between 4.2 and 5.45. Rates in Greece, Austria, and the United Kingdom, Norway, Italy, Switzerland, Spain, and Belgium range between only 1.75 and 2.8.

The same report shows that the United States has 37.2 rapes per 100,000 people. The rate in Sweden is 15.7 and in Denmark, 11.23. Rates in Ireland, Greece, Belgium, Austria, Spain, Luxembourg, Switzerland, France, Finland, the United Kingdom, Norway, and Germany range between only 1.72 and 8.6.

The United States has 221 armed robberies per 100,000 people. Spain tops that with 265. However, rates in Italy, Austria, the United Kingdom, Belgium, France, and Canada are much lower—between 50 and 94.

Such statistics, Ellis contends, shatter the main explanation Bainbridge and Stark give for their contention that religion inhibits crimes. Ellis classifies their explanation as "group solidarity." It goes like this: those who participate in organized religion are members of a group that by definition does not condone crime. Therefore, they will be less likely to commit crimes.

Refuting Theories About Religion and Crime Control

Group solidarity is the most common explanation given by those who view religion as a barrier to crime, Ellis discovered after analyzing more than fifty studies on the relationship between religion and criminality. He pinpointed three other explanations given by researchers.

One Ellis calls "coincidental." According to this theory, religious people just happen to have social status or education levels that make them less likely to commit crimes. And non-religious people just happen to have other variables in their lives—such as drug use or frequent moves—that make them commit more crimes.

Ellis terms another theory "the Hell Fire explanation." It applies to those religions that hold as a tenet an afterlife in which one pays for sins committed in life. Logically, this explanation goes, members of such churches would be less likely to commit crimes. Ellis notes, however, that counterbalancing such a threat is the fact that religions—such as Catholicism—that expound such theories also offer readily available absolution. That makes the real threat of hellfire remote.

Finally, Ellis identifies the "obedience-to-authority theory." This argues simply that those who are members of organized religions exhibit strong willingness to submit to authority and are eager to do as told. Hence, they would be less likely to commit crimes that might anger the authority figure.

While dismissing each of those explanations as faulty, Ellis is embarking on research into neurohormonal explanations of human behavior. He is trying to learn whether "arousal theory"—the theory that a person's need for arousal leads to certain behaviors—can explain crime.

An Alternate Theory About Church and Crime

Linking the theory to studies of religion and criminality, Ellis suggests that those who can sit through church services have average levels of arousal. They do not need to engage in activities to get themselves aroused or excited. So, they may not commit as many crimes.

On the other hand, those who cannot sit still for church services may have suboptimal arousal. They may need to engage in stimulating behavior, including crimes, to reach normal arousal levels. This research could support the view that it is not religion in itself that daunts crime. Rather, certain

> *"It is not religion in itself that daunts crime."*

characteristics related to the activities surrounding religion happen to attract non-criminals. These activities include obedience and frequent attendance at church services.

The need for such research is becoming critical because the outcries to fight crime become more strident every year.

The *Manchester Guardian* recently quoted the Archbishop of Canterbury, George Carey. He said that atheists cannot fully understand goodness and are less likely than believers to do good deeds without personal reward.

To cut crime and boost morality, clerics such as the Archbishop and laypeople such as Colson are choosing what may be a perilously wrong weapon—religion.

Chapter 2

Is Crime Increasing?

Chapter Preface

Crime rates from across the nation are compiled yearly in two government re-ports: the FBI's Uniform Crime Reports and the Bureau of Justice Statistics' Crime Victimization Survey. The FBI counts the number of crimes reported to police each year, while the BJS asks thousands of people whether they have been the victim of a crime within the past year.

While these official statistics show that rates of violent crime have decreased by some measure during the 1990s, many commentators maintain that the over-all crime problem is still extremely serious. Francis Mancini, a columnist for the *Providence (R.I.) Journal-Bulletin,* contends that crime rates are still much higher than they were in the early 1960s. The crime rate must decline to the lev-els of the 1960s, he argues, before the situation can be considered acceptable. "We must not allow ourselves to get accustomed to the current high rates of criminal violence," Mancini asserts.

Others, however, maintain that the crime problem is no worse now than it has ever been. For example, Morris Thigpen, director of the National Institute of Corrections, points out that the murder rate is actually one-tenth of a percentage point lower than it was in the early 1970s, meaning that an average person's chance of becoming a murder victim is nearly exactly the same as it was then. Thigpen blames the media for creating the incorrect impression that crime rates are unacceptably high. "On the basis of what we see and hear, we tend to be-lieve murders are skyrocketing," he states. In his opinion, though, the statistics prove that such worries are unfounded.

In predicting future crime trends, criminologists look at many variables, in-cluding past crime rates and the numbers of teenagers in the population (since teenagers usually commit the most crimes). The viewpoints in the following chapter explore the significance of these variables in debating whether crime is increasing or decreasing.

Crime Is Increasing

by Adam Walinsky

About the author: *Adam Walinsky is a lawyer and a long-time advocate of the Police Corps, which trains students to become police officers.*

All through 1993 official agencies claimed that crime was declining. The FBI said that violent crime in the first six months was down three percent overall, and down eight percent in the Northeast.

One Long Descending Night

For crime to be down even eight percent would mean that a precinct that had had a hundred murders in 1992 had ninety-two in 1993. But nobody came around on New Year's Day of 1993 to give everyone's memory a rinse, obliterating the horrors of the previous year. The effect is not disjunctive but cumulative. By the end of 1993, ninety-two additional people had been murdered.

Many people can also remember years before 1992, in large cities and in small. In 1960, for example, six murders, four rapes, and sixteen robberies were reported in New Haven, Connecticut. In 1990 that city, with a population 14 percent smaller, had thirty-one murders, 168 rapes, and 1,784 robberies: robbery increased more than 100 times, or *10,000 percent*, over thirty years. In this perspective a one-year decrease of seven percent would seem less than impressive.

New Haven is not unique. In Milwaukee in 1965 there were twenty-seven murders, thirty-three rapes, and 214 robberies, and in 1990, when the city was smaller, there were 165 murders, 598 rapes, and 4,472 robberies: robbery became twenty-one times as frequent in twenty-five years. New York City in 1951 had 244 murders; every year for more than a decade it has had nearly 2,000 murders.

We experience the crime wave not as separate moments in time but as one long descending night. A loved one lost echoes in the heart for decades. Every working police officer knows the murder scene: the shocked family and neighbors, too numb yet to grieve; fear and desolation spreading to the street, the workplace, the school, the home, creating an invisible but indelible network of anguish and loss. We have experienced more than 20,000 such scenes every year for more than a decade, and few of them have been truly forgotten.

From Adam Walinsky, "The Crisis of Public Order," *Atlantic Monthly,* July 1995. Reprinted by permission of the author.

The memory of a mugging may fade but does not vanish. Nine percent of those responding to a recent poll in *New York Newsday* said that they had been mugged or assaulted in the past year. This suggests an annual total for the city of more than 600,000 muggings and assaults (remember also that many people, in poor neighborhoods especially, are assaulted more than once). That would be four times as many robberies and assaults as are reported to the police department. The Department of Justice says that not three quarters but only half of all violent crimes go unreported: it may be that many report as having happened "last year" an incident from more than a year ago.

Nevertheless, these are stunning numbers, especially when some other common crimes are added in. Eight percent of those polled (implying 560,000 New Yorkers) said their houses or apartments had been broken into; 22 percent (1,540,000) said their cars had been broken into. In all, 42 percent (nearly three million New Yorkers) said they had been the victims of crime in 1993. And, of course, about 2,000 were murdered. This is what it means to say that crime in 1993 was down eight percent.

In October of 1994 the Bureau of Justice Statistics reported that violent crime had not, after all, declined in 1993 but had risen by 5.6 percent.

Several years ago the Department of Justice estimated that 83 percent of all Americans would be victims of violent crime at least once in their lives. About a quarter would be victims of three or more violent crimes. We are progressing steadily toward the fulfillment of that prediction.

The Numbers of Murders That Are Solved

Our greatest fear is of violence from a nameless, faceless stranger. Officials have always reassured citizens by stating that the great majority of murders, at any rate, are committed by a relative or an acquaintance of the victim's; a 1993 Department of Justice report said the figure for 1988 was eight out of ten.

Unfortunately, that report described only murders in which the killer was known to prosecutors and an arrest was made. It did not mention that more and more killers remain unknown and at liberty after a full police investigation; every year the police make arrests in a smaller proportion of murder cases. In our largest cities the police now make arrests in fewer than three out of five murder cases. In other words, two out of every five killers are completely untouched by the law.

> *"We have experienced more than 20,000 [murder] scenes every year for more than a decade, and few of them have been truly forgotten."*

When a killing is a family tragedy, or takes place between friends or acquaintances, the police make an arrest virtually every time. When the police make an arrest, they say that the crime has been "cleared"; the percentage of crimes for which they make arrests is referred to as the clearance rate. Because murder has historically been a matter principally among families and friends, the homicide clearance rate in the past was often greater than 95 percent, even in the largest cities. As late as 1965 the national homicide clearance rate was 91 percent. However, as crime has spread and changed its character over the past generation, clearance rates have steadily dropped. Between 1993 and 1995 the national homicide clearance rate averaged 65.5 percent. The rate in the sixty-two largest cities is 60.5 percent. In the very largest cities—those with populations over a million—the rate is 58.3 percent.

The Truth About Murders by Strangers

The missing killers are almost certainly not family members, friends, or neighbors. Rather, they are overwhelmingly strangers to their victims, and their acts are called "stranger murders." Here is the true arithmetic: The 40 percent of killings in which city police departments are unable to identify and arrest perpetrators must overwhelmingly be counted as stranger murders; let us assume that 90 percent of them

> *"Every year the police make arrests in a smaller proportion of murder cases."*

are committed by killers unknown to the victims. That number is equivalent to 36 percent of the total of all city murders. We know that of the 60 percent of killers the police do succeed in arresting, 20 percent have murdered strangers. That is, they have committed 12 percent of all murders. As best we can count, then, at least 48 percent of city murders are now being committed by killers who are not relatives or acquaintances of the victims.

This simple arithmetic has been available to the government and its experts for years. However, the first government document to acknowledge these facts was the FBI's annual report on crime in the United States for 1993, which was released in December 1994. The FBI now estimates that 53 percent of all homicides are being committed by strangers. For more than two decades, as homicide clearance rates have plummeted, law-enforcement agencies have continued to assure the public that four fifths of all killings are the result of personal passions. Thus were we counseled to fear our loved ones above all, to regard the family hearth as the most dangerous place. Now that falsehood has been unmasked: the FBI tells us that actually 12 percent of all homicides take place within the family. I have heard no public official anywhere in the United States say a word about any of this.

The Odds of Being Arrested for Murder

There is another important aspect to the arithmetic: the odds facing a robber or holdup man as he decides whether to let his victim live. Again, at least 48 percent of city homicides are stranger murders, but only 12 percent of city homicides result in arrest. That is, the odds that a holdup man who kills a stranger will be arrested appear to be one in four. The Department of Justice tells us that of all those who are arrested for murder, 73 percent will be convicted of some crime; and when convicted, the killers of strangers tend to get the heaviest penalties. Nevertheless, the cumulative chances of getting clean away with the murder of a stranger are greater than 80 percent. Street thugs may be smarter than they are usually given credit for being. They do not consult government reports, but they appear to know the facts. New York bodega workers have experienced an increasing incidence of holdups ending in murder even when they have offered no resistance. Killing eliminates the possibility of witness identification.

Murder is the most frightening crime, but is the least common. Much more frequent are robbery and assault. Robbery, the forcible taking of property from the person of the victim, is the crime most likely to be committed by a stranger; 75 percent of victims are robbed by strangers. Aggravated assault, the use of a weapon or other major force with the intention of causing serious bodily harm, is the most common violent crime; 58 percent of aggravated assaults are committed by strangers.

Interracial and Intraracial Violence

Attacks across racial lines are a special case of crimes by strangers. Most crimes, including 80 percent of violent crimes, are committed by persons of the same race as their victims. However, the experiences of blacks and whites diverge in some respects. In cases involving a lone offender, 56 percent of white and Hispanic robbery victims report that their assailant was white or Hispanic and 40 percent that he was black. When two or more robbers commit the crime, white and Hispanic victims 38 percent of the time report them to be white or Hispanic, 46 percent of the time black, and 10 percent of the time mixed. About eight percent of black victims, in contrast, are robbed by whites or Hispanics, and more than 85 percent by blacks, whether the offenders are alone or in groups. Blacks and whites are robbed equally—75 percent of the time—by strangers, but as these figures indicate, whites are far more likely to be robbed by strangers of a different race.

> *"The FBI now estimates that 53 percent of all homicides are being committed by strangers."*

This result occurs because there are many more white people and many more white victims: 87 percent of all violent crimes are committed against whites and Hispanics. In robberies lone white offenders select white victims 96 percent of the time, and lone black offenders select white victims 62 percent of the time. White rapists select white victims 97 percent of the time; black rapists select white victims 48 percent of the time. Whites committing aggravated assault attack blacks in three percent of cases; blacks commit about half their assaults against whites.

When all violent crimes are taken together, 58 percent of white victims and 54 percent of black victims report that their assailant was a stranger. Citizens of all races who are fearful of random violence have good reason for their concern. Storekeepers, utility workers, police officers, and ordinary citizens out for a carton of milk or a family dinner are all increasingly at risk. . . .

The Role of Rising Illegitimacy Rates

In 1965 Daniel Patrick Moynihan warned that a growing proportion of black children were being born to single mothers. When such large numbers of children were abandoned by their fathers and brought up by single mothers, he said, the result was sure to be wild violence and social chaos. He was excoriated as a racist and the subject was abandoned. The national rate of illegitimacy among blacks that year was 26 percent.

It took just over a decade for the black illegitimacy rate to reach 50 percent. And in 1990, twenty-five years after Moynihan's warning, two thirds of black children were born to single mothers, many of them teenagers. Only a third of black children lived with both parents even in the first three years of their lives. Seven percent of all black children and five percent of black children under the age of three were living with neither a father nor a mother in the house. The rate of illegitimacy more than doubled in one generation.

Social disorder—in its many varieties, and with the assistance of government policies—can perhaps be said to have caused the sudden collapse of family institutions and social bonds that have survived three centuries of slavery and oppression. It is at any rate certain that hundreds of thousands of the children so abandoned have become in their turn a major cause of instability. Most notably they have tended to commit crimes, especially violent crimes, out of all proportion to their numbers. Of all juveniles confined for violent offenses today, less than 30 percent grew up with both parents.

How many killers are there, and who are they? In 1990 a total of 24,932 homicides were reported. Of all killers identified by the nation's police forces and reported to the Department of Justice for that year, 43.7 percent were white and Hispanic and 54.7 percent were black. Whites made up 83.9 percent of the population that year, and blacks 12.3 percent. The rate of homicide committed by whites was thus 5.2 per 100,000, and by blacks 44.7 per 100,000—or about eight times as great. In the large counties analyzed by the Department of Justice, 62 percent of identified killers were black. This is equivalent to a black homicide rate of 50.7 per 100,000—close to ten times the rate among other citizens. Serial killers and mass murderers, however, are overwhelmingly white.

> *"The cumulative chances of getting clean away with the murder of a stranger are greater than 80 percent."*

Of the urban killers identified by the Department of Justice in 1988, 90 percent were male. Virtually none were aged fourteen or younger, but 16 percent were aged fifteen to nineteen, 24 percent were twenty to twenty-four, and 20 percent were twenty-five to twenty-nine.

The white and black populations each suffered about 12,000 homicides in 1990. But the black population base is smaller, and the rate at which blacks fall victim is much higher. The victimization rate for white males was 9.0 per 100,000, and for white females 2.8 per 100,000. For black males it was an astonishing 69.2, and for black females it was 13.5. According to the Department of Justice, one out of every twenty-one black men can expect to be murdered. This is a death rate double that of American servicemen in the Second World War.

The Crime Wave to Come

Prospects for the future are apparent in the facts known about children already born. This is what Senator Moynihan means when he says the next thirty years are "already spoken for."

We first notice the children of the ghetto when they grow muscles—at about the age of fifteen. The children born in 1965 reached their fifteenth year in 1980, and 1980 and 1981 set new records for criminal violence in the United States, as teenage and young adult blacks ripped at the fabric of life in the black inner city. Nevertheless, of all the black children who reached physical maturity in those years, three quarters had been born to a married mother and father. Not until 1991 did we experience the arrival in their mid-teens of the first group of black youths fully half of whom had been born to single mothers—the cohort born in 1976. Criminal violence particularly associated with young men and boys reached new peaks of destruction in black communities in 1990 and 1991.

In the year 2000 the black youths born in 1985 will turn fifteen. Three fifths of them were born to single mothers, many of whom were drug-addicted; one in fourteen will have been raised with neither parent at home; unprecedented numbers will have been subjected to beatings and other abuse; and most will have grown up amid the utter chaos pervading black

"Citizens of all races who are fearful of random violence have good reason for their concern."

city neighborhoods. It is supremely necessary to change the conditions that are producing such cohorts. But no matter what efforts we now undertake, we have already assured the creation of more very violent young men than any reasonable society can tolerate, and their numbers will grow inexorably for every one of the next twenty years.

In absolute numbers the teenage and young adult population aged fifteen to twenty-four stagnated or actually declined over the past decade. Crime has been rising because this smaller population has grown disproportionately more violent. Now it is about to get larger in size. James Fox, a dean at Northeastern University, in Boston, has shown that from 1965 to 1985 the national homicide rate tracked almost exactly the proportion of the population aged eighteen to twenty-four. Suddenly, in 1985, the two curves diverged sharply. The number of young adults as a proportion of the population declined; but the overall homicide rate went up, because among this smaller group the homicide rate increased by 65 percent in just eight years. Among those aged fourteen to seventeen, the next group of young adults, the homicide rate more than doubled. What we experienced from 1985 on was a conjunction of two terrible arrivals. One train carried the legacy of the 1970s, the children of the explosion of illegitimacy and paternal abandonment. Crack arrived on the same timetable, and unloaded at the same station.

Fox shows further that by the year 2005 the population aged fourteen to seventeen will have increased by a

> *"Of all juveniles confined for violent offenses today, less than 30 percent grew up with both parents."*

remarkable 23 percent. Professor John DiIulio, of Princeton University, predicts that the number of homicides may soon rise to 35,000 or 40,000 a year, with other violent offenses rising proportionally. Fox calls what we are about to witness an "epidemic" of teenage crime. He does not give a name to our present condition. . . .

Beyond the Numbers

For more than twenty years the children of the ghetto have witnessed violent death as an almost routine occurrence. They have seen it on their streets, in their schools, in their families, and on TV. They have lived with constant fear. Many have come to believe that they will not live to see twenty-five. These are often children whose older brothers, friends, and uncles have taught them that only the strong and the ruthless survive. Prison does not frighten them—it is a rite of passage that a majority of their peers may have experienced. Too many have learned to kill without remorse, for a drug territory or for an insult, because of a look or a bump on the sidewalk, or just to do it: why not?

These young people have been raised in the glare of ceaseless media violence and incitement to every depravity of act and spirit. Movies may feature scores of killings in two hours' time, vying to show methods ever more horrific; many are quickly imitated on the street. Television commercials teach that a young man requires a new pair of $120 sneakers each week. Major corporations make and sell records exhorting their listeners to brutalize Koreans, rob store owners, rape women, kill the police. Ashamed and guilt-ridden, elite opinion often encourages even hoodlums to carry a sense of entitlement and grievance against society and its institutions.

These lessons are being taught to millions of children as I write and you read. They have already been taught to the age groups that will reach physical maturity during the rest of this century.

The worst lesson we have taught these benighted children I have saved for last, because it is a lesson we have also taught ourselves: We will do almost anything not to have to act to defend ourselves, our country, or our character as people of decency and strength. We have fled from our cities, virtually abandoning great institutions such as the public schools. We have permitted the spread within our country of wastelands ruled not by the Constitution and lawful authority but by the anarchic force of merciless killers. We have muted our dialogue and hidden our thoughts. We have abandoned millions of our fellow citizens—people of decency and honor trying desperately to raise their children in love and hope—to every danger and degraded assault. We have become isolated from one another, dispirited about any possibility of collective or political action to meet this menace. We shrink in fear of teenage thugs on every street. More important, we shrink even from contemplating the forceful collective action we know is required. We abandon our self-respect and our responsibility to ourselves and our posterity.

How to change all this, how to recover heart and spirit, how to save the lives and souls of millions of children, and how to save ourselves from this scourge of violent anarchy—in short, how to deal with things as they are, how to respond to the implacable and undeniable numbers: this will be the real measure and test of our political system. But more than that, it will be the measure of our own days and work, the test of our own lives and heritage.

Violent Crime Is Increasing

by Michael Hedges

About the author: *Michael Hedges is a national reporter for the* Washington Times.

Each person's chances of being set upon by violent thugs and robbed, killed, or raped grow each year. The number of Americans altering their behavior—avoiding night activities, eschewing automated teller machines, staying away from downtown areas even if it means missing a play, ballet, or basketball game—is at an all-time high, according to behavioral experts.

Violent Crime Increases Each Decade

Some statistics, such as the murder rate in Washington, D.C., bear out the apprehension with which people face the world. The brutality of crime increases almost exponentially each decade, so that what once horrified us we now accept as sadly routine.

"The climate is changing," says Dennis Martin, a former police chief who is president of the National Association of Chiefs of Police. "We are working on a comprehensive study with Columbia University that shows our attitudes have clearly changed. We have become almost desensitized to crime and violence."

In a study involving 374 mayors or municipal executives from cities with populations over 10,000, the National League of Cities found a growing sense of unease among those living in urban or suburban areas.

For 1993, more than 4 in 10 felt violent crime had worsened in their city in the past year. Another 5 in 10 thought the number of gangs involved in criminal activity had grown. Only 2 in 10 thought violent crime had lessened, and fewer than 1 in 10 believed their cities were less at risk from gangs.

The increase in the number of civic officials who admitted their crime was worsening was greater than in any other year in the past decade.

The study Martin worked on contains an analysis of how college students respond to violent imagery. "The reaction to violence by young people today is significantly different than it was in 1960," he says.

Martin echoes the sentiments of other current and former law enforcement officials as he catalogs reasons why.

Early release of criminals. "One thing we are finding is that when someone is arrested for burglary today, he has committed between 40 and 100 previous crimes," says Martin. "That makes effective law enforcement impossible."

Proliferation of plea bargaining. "Offenses are being bargained down because of prosecutors' work loads and lack of jail space, until the punishment bears no resemblance to the

> *"The brutality of crime increases almost exponentially each decade, so that what once horrified us we now accept as sadly routine."*

crime," says Martin. "What you too often see is a violent criminal accepting a plea to a nonviolent offense, so he gets paroled quickly. The next time he's arrested he doesn't have a prior history as a violent felon, so he gets another deal."

Lack of values and education. "Four out of five people convicted of serious crimes never finished high school," he says. "If a person has been physically abused by his parents, his chances of being a criminal double."

Breakdown in respect for authority. "The way people view authority figures has changed remarkably since the early 1960s," says Martin. "Our figures show the number of assaults each year on police officers has risen 846 percent since 1960."

Is Everyone Affected by Crime?

That is the stark view of what is happening: A system that can't catch and hold criminals or protect the innocent is being confronted with a rising tide of increasingly violent youths who have failed to learn, either from their families or society, how to behave. But does this situation lead to well-advised caution or panic? Are our perceptions of crime and the average person's safety accurate?

Law enforcement experts at every level—as well as the blizzard of statistics put together by the U.S. Justice Department, state agencies, and others—indicate the answers depend on who you are, where you live, and how you live your life.

Dewey Stokes, president of the National Fraternal Order of Police, says, "The heinous crimes the news media are attracted to have come to the forefront. Sometimes it seems to me there is almost a sense of one-upmanship among these violent psychopaths."

All agree that there is far too much crime in America, more than in other civilized nations. But the sense that the country is under siege by criminals, which has mushroomed since the 1970s, may be an exaggeration. The perception is fueled by media ability to put us on the scene of violence and, ironically, by improvements in the way police investigate and document crime.

To illustrate, think back to the mid-1970s, a time many might view as an age of innocence compared to today. In fact, your chances of being robbed or burglarized were greater in 1976 than in 1992, according to statistics compiled by the Justice Department. By the early 1980s, some categories of violent crime, such as rape, had peaked.

The percentage of households in the United States experiencing any kind of crime dropped from 32 to 26 percent from the mid-1970s to 1992. But the story is different if you move the time frame backward: Violent crime has risen dramatically compared to 30 years ago.

In 1960, the chances of being murdered or a victim of intentional manslaughter were 5 in 100,000 for Americans. The chances of being raped were 10 per 100,000 and of being assaulted about 86 per 100,000. In 1991, these figures had risen to almost 9 murders or manslaughters, 42 rapes, and 433 aggravated assaults per 100,000. The overall chances of being in a violent crime have risen about 600 percent since 1960, from 161 to 758 per 100,000.

A Decrease in Robberies, but an Increase in Violent Crime

"There is a decrease in some categories, such as house and business burglaries," says Stokes. "In some areas, there has been a drop in armed robberies.

"But what you are seeing is an increase in violent crime and drug crimes in some areas where it becomes a high-profile phenomenon," he says. "For example, there have been increases in rape reports around major universities. In some suburban areas drug gangs have moved in seeking new markets, and there has been an accompanying surge in all the associated crimes: murders, robberies, drug arrests." The spread of drug-peddling organizations from cities to suburban areas has contributed to many Americans' feeling that nobody is safe.

Stokes, who monitors crime from all over the country, says it has become much more common for police in rural and suburban areas to end up in a shootout with a drug criminal.

> *"All agree that there is far too much crime in America, more than in other civilized nations."*

"These drug dealers are not afraid of apprehension, because they understand that the way the system is set up they won't have to do more than 10 to 35 percent of the time they are given," he says. "We call these groups gangs like they were a bunch of teenagers banding together to defend their turf. What we should call them is organized crime. They are groups of criminals between 14 and 35 years old organized to make money by setting up criminal operations."

Safest Places to Live

Based on an array of statistics and information from law enforcement officers nationwide, Stokes has compiled a list of places he would still rate as safe.

"There aren't too many in the northeast quadrant," he says. "There used to be a few in Maryland, deep in South Carolina. Right now I'd say most of Wyoming and Idaho, quite a bit of the Dakotas. Colorado used to be safe, but

Denver is not anymore, and there are problems in Fort Collins."

In other words, areas of low population density in the Far West. "When there is a more sparsely populated area, people depend on each other more. There is a better sense of community, and they are more wary of strangers," he says.

But the perception that the West is more crime free than elsewhere doesn't stand up under statistical analysis. According to the comprehensive Justice Department figures, one's chances of being a victim of any crime are highest in the West.

Those figures measure the number of households in which one or more people are victimized by any crime, no matter how petty, in a given year. By region, the 1992 numbers were 18 percent for the Northeast, 20.9 percent for the Midwest, 23.4 percent for the South, and 28.5 percent for the West.

The numbers of those falling prey to a "serious violent crime"—as the Justice Department characterizes a rape, robbery, or aggravated assault—are much smaller but show a similar breakdown by region: Northeast 4.7 percent, Midwest 6.3 percent, South 7.2 percent, and West 9.1 percent.

The Least Safe Place to Live

The FBI publishes a state-by-state crime analysis each year that also includes the District of Columbia. That analysis for 1992 shows that Washington, D.C., was by far the most dangerous spot, at least when compared with states, where rural, suburban, and urban populations coexist.

The FBI Uniform Crime Reporting Program estimates crimes in various categories per 100,000 inhabitants. Its broadest index contains three categories:

• A total crime index, which measures the sum of all murders, manslaughter, forcible rape, robbery, aggravated assault, burglary, larceny, and car theft.

• A violent crime index, which counts murder, rape, armed robbery, and assault.

• Property crimes, including burglary, theft, nonviolent robbery, and car theft.

The FBI figures indicate that 10,768 out of every 100,000 inhabitants of Washington, D.C., were crime victims in 1992. North Dakota had the lowest overall crime rate by this measure, 2,793 per 100,000.

"Violent crime has risen dramatically compared to 30 years ago."

"That is accurate but somewhat misleading," says a federal law enforcement expert. "Washington is probably more accurately compared to Houston, New York, Los Angeles, or Chicago, other major urban centers."

Washington also had the highest figures for violent crime. At 2,453 crimes per 100,000 inhabitants, Washington was more than twice as violent as the next most afflicted area, Florida, which had 1,184 reported acts of violence for every 100,000. California, New York, and Illinois all had violent crime rates of 1,000 per 100,000 or more. North Dakota was the least violent place, with 65 violent crimes per 100,000. Next was Vermont, with 117.

New Hampshire, South Dakota, West Virginia, Maine, Montana, Utah, Idaho, Iowa, Wisconsin, Wyoming, and Hawaii had violent crime rates of about 300 or less per 100,000.

> *"The places Americans feel safe are in danger of disappearing, if not in fact, then in the minds of citizens."*

For property crime, again, Washington, D.C., was the worst place to live, with 8,315 such offenses per 100,000 inhabitants. Florida and Texas were second and third, with 7,363 and 6,979 per 100,000. Arizona, which had a moderate rate for violent crime, is fourth in terms of frequency of property crimes, with 6,735 per 100,000.

Kentucky, South Dakota, North Dakota, New Hampshire, West Virginia, Pennsylvania, Montana, Maine, Vermont, Iowa, Idaho, and Mississippi had property crime rates under 4,000 per 100,000 inhabitants.

The Justice Department put together a list of populated areas that were low in crime. The five safest moderately populated areas in America in 1992 were Wheeling, West Virginia; Beaver County, Pennsylvania (northeast of Pittsburgh); Cumberland, Maryland; St. Cloud, Minnesota; and Johnstown, Pennsylvania. But the places Americans feel safe are in danger of disappearing, if not in fact, then in the minds of citizens.

Crime Reports Contribute to Fear

With grim regularity, reports are issued documenting another aspect of a violent world. That information is digested and regurgitated by the media, adding another aspect to the perception of fear.

In January 1994, for example, a survey conducted by the Justice Department's Bureau of Justice Statistics found that approximately 2.5 million of the nation's 107 million females 12 years old and older were raped, robbed, or assaulted in a typical year, or were the victim of a threat or an attempt to commit such a crime.

Nearly a third, 28 percent, of those making the assaults or threats were the women's husbands or boyfriends. Another 40 percent were relatives or acquaintances. The survey tended to argue against the image of the shadowy stranger as rapist and put the onus on those the women knew and loved.

Violent crime has been building for years and is now regarded by many Americans as the country's greatest problem. As such it promises to be a political cause célèbre through the 1996 elections and beyond.

The Increasing Fear of Crime Is Justified

by Terry Golway

About the author: *Terry Golway is a columnist for* America, *a weekly Jesuit publication.*

The corner of 105th Street and Amsterdam Avenue on Manhattan's West Side seems an innocuous enough place as urban areas go. It has its immigrant-run shops, its working-class families and its ever-present vagrants. Children wearing backpacks scamper across the busy street every morning on their way to the local public school around the block. In morning's light it seems an unremarkable, workaday urban neighborhood.

Danger Even in Normal Neighborhoods

So it is. But even unremarkable neighborhoods are fraught with hidden dangers these days. A few weeks ago, 9-year-old John Valentine was on his way to school when the sidewalk turned into a free-fire zone. Little John had walked into the middle of a gun battle between two gangs of drug dealers. John was the only casualty, falling to the cold sidewalk when a bullet hit him in the right shoulder and passed through his chest. Another day, another casualty in the low-intensity war that takes place in our very backyards.

John Valentine survived, but his awful story serves as a reminder that despite rumors to the contrary, you still have to be careful out there in America.

The generals who are fighting America's war on crime assure us not only that there is light at the tunnel's end, but that tranquil, sunlit uplands await our arrival. Their optimism is not without cause. Crime rates are falling faster than General Motors sales figures of two decades ago. If crime were an industry, frenzied brokers would be bailing out and economists would be talking about the need for crime bosses to downsize their operations in order to compete in the global marketplace.

Certainly the numbers are astonishing. Most major American cities are seeing annual, double-digit decreases in major crimes, which led at least one slick ur-

From Terry Golway, "Life in the 90s." Originally published in the February 24, 1996, issue of *America.* Reprinted with the permission of Terry Golway and America Press, Inc., 106 W. 56th St., New York, NY 10019.

ban magazine, ever ready to announce the arrival of a trend, to pronounce an end to crime as we know it. In New York, murders have declined by nearly half in the last five years. No wonder the city's Police Commissioner, William Bratton, is being hailed as the George Patton of the war on crime.

Decreasing Crime, but Increasing Worry

The good news about crime comes at a time when the airwaves are filled with lurid advertisements offering no end of personal safety products, which suggests that not everybody is buying into the end-of-crime theory. The Federal Bureau of Investigation's statistics may sound reassuring, but the stores in my neck of the woods can't stock enough anti-car theft devices, and lately I've noticed the local hardware store displaying handy-dandy spray cans of Mace and some other nasty concoction that looks like it could drop an elephant at 30 paces.

The newspapers, too, are filled with pitches from home security specialists, who apparently have every reason to believe there is a lucrative market of trembling homeowners out there. The end of crime as we know it? Tell that to the folks who just spent a couple of thousand dollars wiring their little patch of God's good earth.

The politicians and bureaucrats who are lining up to take credit for falling crime rates don't dare say what everyone else knows perfectly well to be the truth. The recent drop in crime, however welcome, is something like the Northeast's most recent winter storm. Coming two weeks after the region was buried under 28 inches, well, a mere 10 inches seemed like the end of winter as we knew it.

> *"The Federal Bureau of Investigation's statistics may sound reassuring, but the stores in my neck of the woods can't stock enough anti-car theft devices."*

New York's murder rate illustrates the point. The drop in murders from 2,245 in 1990 to 1,182 in 1995, of course, is terrific news. The city ought to give thanks to its Police Department and its public officials.

But still . . . 1,182 murders! No city on earth would regard such a figure as worthy of celebration, unless, of course, the earlier number had been even higher. But where else on earth, save America's gun-addicted inner cities, would a nation at peace tolerate such a terrible body count among its citizens?

In 1995, a year celebrated for its relative saftey, New York produced about a third as many corpses as Northern Ireland has produced in a quarter-century of a small-scale insurrection. Until recently, it seemed a journalistic rule that nobody could write about Belfast without first affixing the adjective "war-torn." But I have walked the troubled streets of Belfast and felt safer than I have even in some of New York's choicest neighborhoods. I know immigrants from Belfast who tell stories of walking home in the wee hours without ever listening for footsteps behind them or wondering who might be lurking around the corner. They dare not do that in New York or Boston, they say.

Not an End to Crime

The good news about crime should not shroud the unpleasant truth that end-of-century America remains a terribly violent place, a nation of a million prisoners and millions of crimes. If it seems a little less violent than a few years ago, that is cause for further study, not celebration.

Even as I write this, the all-news radio playing in the background is giving updates on a terrible story unfolding in East Orange, N.J. A clergyman, the announcer is saying, has been gravely wounded in a carjacking. A hospital spokesman reports that the victim's family has been summoned to his bedside.

The end to crime as we know it? Only if you live in fantasy land.

Violent Crime Is Not Increasing

by Richard Moran

About the author: *Richard Moran is a professor of sociology and criminology at Mount Holyoke College in South Hadley, Massachusetts.*

Meteorologists add the wind-chill factor to their winter weather forecasts to make the actual temperature seem worse than it is. Likewise, when the F.B.I. reported [in May 1996] that serious crime had declined slightly for the fourth year in a row, it was still making the statistics sound worse than they actually were. That's because the Government tends to exaggerate the violent nature of crime.

How Violent Is Violent Crime?

According to the Justice Department's Bureau of Justice Statistics, less than a third of the 6.6 million violent crimes committed in the United States in 1992 (the last year for which statistics are available) resulted in injury; most of the victims suffered only minor cuts, scratches or bruises. About 20 percent of them needed minor medical care; 7 percent went to emergency rooms. Only 1 percent of the victims were hurt seriously enough to require hospitalization.

The incongruity arises because of the way the law defines violent crime. For example, aggravated assault is defined as either intentionally causing serious bodily harm or using a weapon to threaten or attempt to cause bodily harm. Fortunately, most aggravated assaults fall into the last category; most victims are never touched by the offender.

The same holds true for armed robbery. In 1992, less than a third of robbery victims were injured and only 3 percent required medical treatment. Less than half of armed robbers displayed guns, and those who did were less likely to injure victims than robbers who didn't show guns.

Exaggerated Crime Statistics

Yet the F.B.I. has a tendency to worry people unnecessarily, even when it has good news. [In 1995], it announced that 53 percent of all homicides were committed by strangers, and that for the first time all Americans had a "realistic" chance of being murdered. But to arrive at these troubling figures, the F.B.I. considered all unsolved homicides, including drug-related killings, as homicides committed by strangers, thus creating an impression that murder was becoming increasingly random.

The push for "three strikes" laws has also helped exaggerate the violent nature of crime. By combining disparate categories of offenders under such categories as "violent," "persistent" and "serious," these laws fail to distinguish the habitual petty criminal from more vicious felons. Under Federal law and the laws of California and Washington State, drug trafficking, burglary and prostitution are considered violent crimes.

> *"An American's chances of being murdered are no greater today than they were two decades ago."*

An American's chances of being murdered are no greater today than they were two decades ago. It was 1 in 10,500 in 1993 compared with 1 in 10,200 in 1974. For those aged 50 and over, the risk has dropped sharply. (The notable exception is the homicide rate among black male teenagers; it has tripled in the past decade.)

This is not to say that violent crime is not a serious problem or to discount the sufferings of the victims. But by offering a more accurate description of violent crime, the Government can help calm fears and encourage a more rational discussion of crime.

The Extent of Crime Has Been Exaggerated by the Media

by John Stossel

About the author: *John Stossel is a reporter for ABC News.*

We reporters should be at least embarrassed, if not ashamed, of the way that we have breathlessly hyped almost every threat that comes across our desks. Okay, maybe some have not, but most of us have, much of the time. I'll start with crime. Polls show that many Americans fear crime more than anything else—and why should they not? Gruesome stories lead local news shows night after night. I watch, with grim fascination, grateful that the horror did not happen to me. Any individual story I can slough off as a bizarre aberration; but the repetition takes a toll. Whenever I return to New York City after weeks away, I am more fearful. The late-night walk home—a routine stroll before— now feels ominous; Central Park is suddenly less . . . inviting.

The Media Create the Impression of a Crime Wave

The fear diminishes within a week. Just experiencing my neighborhood reminds me that it is not *that* scary. But while I'm away, absorbing news about the city through television and through newspapers that my office sends me, I'm left with the feeling that the city is a terrifying place. And should I not feel that? After all, the horror stories are real—reporters do not make this stuff up. And we all know that there is much *more* violence now; Politicians and the media have pointed out that crime rates are skyrocketing, especially for violent crime.

But the fact is that crime is *not* rising. Yes, the horror stories are real, but there have always been horrible crimes; what is new today is that there is more reporting about them. To create today's "crime wave," the media have consis-

From John Stossel, "Pandering to Fear," *Jobs and Capital*, Summer 1996. Reprinted by permission of the Milken Institute for Job and Capital Formation, Santa Monica, California.

tently hyped skewed data, while ignoring better statistics that show the crime rate to have stayed about the same. Skeptical? Here are the facts.

The United States gets its crime statistics from two sources: the FBI, which compiles *reported* crime, and the U.S. Justice Department, which surveys people,

> *"To create today's 'crime wave,' the media have consistently hyped skewed data."*

asking, "Were you a victim?" This Justice Department survey finds much *more* crime. That is not surprising because so much crime is never reported. In 1992, for example, the Justice Department reports that 70 out of every 100,000 Americans were raped, while the FBI reports only 43 per 100,000. Justice says 900 of every 100,000 suffered aggravated assault; the FBI says 442 of every 100,000; and so on.

Among crime experts, the higher Justice Department numbers are widely regarded as the more reliable, precisely because Justice takes unreported crime into account. Here is the surprise: The Justice Department data, high as they are, do not show crime getting worse (see Table 1). Between 1980 and 1992, total crime incidents as reported in the Justice Department survey declined over 16 percent, and the rate of violent crime declined over 3 percent.

How the Media Make Crime Seem Worse

Why, then, do we hear so much about the exploding crime rate? Because the media make crime much more visible. Local crime, 30 years ago, was largely a local event. Victims were reluctant to speak out; many were ashamed that they had been victimized. Today, talk-show driven openness compels us to tell everything, and in the heated competition for readers and TV ratings, every "interesting" crime becomes a headline. Such interesting small-town crimes that 30 years ago were local stories now get national headlines.

Adding to the distorted perceptions, reporters, looking for a sexier way to tell

TABLE 1 JUSTICE DEPARTMENT CRIME SURVEY DATA	
(total percent change, 1980–1992)	
Total crime incidents	-16.4
Violent crime incidents	8.0
Violent crime rate	-3.6
Murder rate	N.A.
Rape rate	-22.2
Robbery rate	-10.6
Aggravated assault rate	-3.2

Sources: U.S. Department of Justice; *Bessette Quarterly Report on Crime and Justice, USA*, vol. I, no. 2.

TABLE 2 FBI REPORTED CRIME DATA	
(total percent change, 1980–1992)	
Total crime incidents	7.7
Violent crime incidents	43.7
Violent crime rate	27.0
Murder rate	-8.8
Rape rate	16.3
Robbery rate	5.0
Aggravated assault rate	48.0
Sources: FBI; *Bessette Quarterly Report on Crime and Justice, USA*, vol. I, no. 2.	

the "bigger" story, often quote the FBI data for reported crime. Reported crime has risen sharply (see Table 2), but that does not mean that the actual crime rate has increased. Based on a comparison of Tables 1 and 2, we can conclude that reporting of crime is going up. Why would that be? Possibly because computers are better (reporting is easier than it used to be) and because police departments have figured out that reporting more crimes yields bigger budgets.

Underscoring the dubious nature of the FBI reported crime data is the FBI statistic on murder rates. Most murders are reported, in that with a murder we have a body to account for; it is hard to get *that* wrong. But notice in Table 2 that the murder-rate trend is inconsistent with the ever-rising FBI figures for other crimes, but completely consistent with the Justice Department data in Table 1 that show the various crime rates relatively flat or declining.

Unsurprisingly, the criminologists say that the Justice Department numbers are accurate. Yet we seldom see them quoted. Why? Because they make for a less interesting story. "I was called by a reporter one time . . . who wanted to do a story on crime and trends in crime," says Mark Warr, a criminologist at the University of Texas. "When I told him crime was going down, he said, 'I'm sorry, my editor will not let me report that story. It's not news when crime is going down.'"

Even when reporters do use the more reliable Justice Department data, we mislead by what we leave out. *USA Today* recently reported that the Justice Department said violent crime was up 24 percent (compared

> *"Reported crime has risen sharply, but that does not mean that the actual crime rate has increased."*

to 20 years ago). It was not a lie; the actual number of crimes did increase, *but so did the population.* In fact, over 20 years, the population increased 25 percent, so the probability of an individual's being victimized actually went down slightly. We are a little safer today. You would never know that from the *USA Today* headline: "Violent Crime Up 24%."

Some of the reporting is just wrong. In the 1980s, many activists claimed that at least 50,000 kids were abducted by strangers every year. It was never true; nearly every "abduction" was a child taken by a disgruntled parent in a custody dispute. Yet the press hyped the story for years. At breakfast, milk cartons remind families: "Fear Strangers!" In truth, children are much more likely to be molested or kidnapped by friends or family members, and a hundred times more likely to be injured by cars, bikes, swimming pools, and the like, but that makes for a less dramatic story.

Crime Is a Persistent Problem, Not an Increasing One

I am not suggesting that crime is not a serious problem. In certain neighborhoods, and among certain groups, crime *is* up. If you are a black teenager, the yearly odds of becoming the victim of some violent crime is one in six. That is a crime wave.

Furthermore, since the big baby boom generation is aging, crime rates *should* be dropping, rather than just staying level. This bodes ill for the next decade, when the boomers' kids will reach prime crime-committing age.

> *"Today's news stories imply that crime is exploding. That is simply wrong."*

It is possible that crime today is worse than it was prior to 20 years ago. The Justice Department began its victimization surveys only in 1973, and the evidence about crime is mixed prior to that year. FBI data on murders show significantly fewer killings in the 1940s, 1950s, and 1960s; then crime increased as the baby-boomers hit their late teens. Murder data for the 1930s, however, list more murders per capita than today. It is not clear that life was safer in the "good old days." Nevertheless, today's news stories imply that crime is exploding. That is simply wrong, and reporters repeat the fallacy every day. . . .

America pays a price for our overemotional reporting. People's lives are diminished by fear. When we believe that there is an epidemic of crime, we give up freedom. We invite politicians to pass repressive laws. We go out less at night, we avoid strangers; we cut ourselves off from other people. "What kind of society are we going to have if no one trusts each other?" asks criminologist Warr. "It tears the social fabric apart if we assume that everyone we run into is a criminal."

The people who are most fearful are those who "get out" the least, those who stay home and experience life through the media. For example, although the age group least likely to be victimized by crime is the elderly, surveys show that it is the elderly who are most afraid. "They become hostages in their homes," says Johnny Mack Brown, president of the National Sheriffs Association. "They start barring their windows, locking their doors." Mack has his men visit the elderly to try to convince them that things are not so bad. But it's a hard sell, he says: "People believe what they see in the media."

Crime Is Decreasing

by Patrick McCormick

About the author: *Patrick McCormick is a columnist for* U.S. Catholic, *a monthly Catholic-oriented magazine.*

[In fall 1994], while politicians and candidates of every stripe were falling over themselves trying to prove to concerned voters that they were tougher on crime than their wimpy opponents, I had a slightly more personal encounter with the surprise hot campaign issue of '94. Somebody tried to mug me.

Paying Attention to Crime and Crime Rhetoric

Fortunately, thanks mainly to my assailant's incompetence and a good deal of luck, I escaped unharmed, and he was later apprehended by the local police. Still, though the incident didn't transform me into a conservative or lead to a National Rifle Association membership, I have felt its lingering impact. More than once in the last few months I've jumped at the unexpected sound of running footsteps, or glanced repeatedly over my shoulder on the nightly walk home.

Even more, however, I found myself paying closer attention to the public conversations politicians and their constituents were having about crime in America. Unfortunately I found many of these blistering exchanges—whether attacking opponents for putting too much "fat" in the crime bill, or blasting candidates for being "soft" on crime—just as disturbing as the attempted assault.

All too often politicians and pundits were content to address crime with sound-bite analysis and simplistic solutions, instead of attempting to grasp its real shape and causes or offer solutions that might be both effective and moral. Of course in the heat of a political campaign it may be unreasonable to expect candidates to challenge popular assumptions about this issue or to offer thoughtful analysis and solutions. Still, now that things have calmed down a bit, it might be helpful if we, as citizens and Christians, sat down and critically examined some of our culture's popular beliefs about crime and punishment in America, and see if we really agree with them.

To anyone in 1994 who was following the various polls, talk-show pundits, and migratory patterns of politicians, it seemed clear both that crime had re-

From Patrick McCormick, "Crime in America: Just the Facts, Ma'am," *U.S. Catholic,* March 1995. Reprinted with permission from the author and *U.S. Catholic,* published by Claretian Publications, 205 W. Monroe, Chicago, IL 60606.

71

placed the economy and health care as a hot-button campaign issue and that American popular culture had some fixed beliefs about this issue. First, survey after survey indicated that a growing majority of middle- and upper-class Americans felt concerned about or threatened by crime and perceived themselves to be in the midst of an explosive and increasingly violent crime wave.

Second, popular culture clearly views this crime wave as resulting from both (a) a loss of moral and family values, and (b) the failure of our criminal-justice system (particularly the courts and politicians) to take a "tough stand" on crime. According to popular opinion, criminals—particularly dangerous ones— are coddled by a system that either excuses their outrageous conduct because of some imagined victimization or shortens their prison sentences to a laughable slap on the wrist.

Third, given the source and tone of the alarm being sounded, one would assume that crime in America consisted mainly of an assault on middle- and upper-class Americans by violent strangers and that this recent crime wave was lapping primarily at the shores of suburbia.

> *"When we contrast popular perceptions about crime with some of the statistical information, a significant gap surfaces between the two."*

Finally, as is evident from [the 1994] campaign and the fuss over the crime bill, the most popular answer to the present crisis is to declare a "war on crime" and shift money away from prevention and social programs while investing even more resources in prisons and police. Thus, politicians and voters clamor for stiffer sentences, more cops, and an increasing reliance upon the death penalty.

But although these beliefs seem well entrenched in our corporate psyche, the question remains as to whether all, or even any, of them are true. And indeed it would seem that they are not, for when we contrast popular perceptions about crime with some of the statistical information, a significant gap surfaces between the two.

A Decreasing Crime Rate

To start with, in spite of the fact that there is an alarmingly high level of criminal violence in our inner cities and among our urban poor, a number of studies raise serious questions about popular conceptions regarding an increasing crime rate. For example, although the majority of Americans surveyed believe that both the overall and violent crime rates have increased dramatically since the early '70s, studies cited in the October [15, 1994,] *Economist* show that the overall rate of crime in America has dropped over the past two decades. And even when the increase in violent crimes is adjusted for population growth, there is a per capita decrease in this rate as well.

Indeed, just as [1994] polls were pointing to a heightened fear of crime in middle-class Americans, FBI reports were indicating a drop in national crime rates. So whatever is spurring this recent concern, it doesn't seem to be a sudden outbreak in the rate of crime in our streets.

Prison Policies and the Crime Rate

Nor does it seem to be true that America coddles its criminals. In spite of the media hype given to high profile "abuse excuse" homicide cases, an article in the conservative journal *Reason* notes that courts are not normally persuaded by such insanity pleas and such defendants are not often acquitted. Also, with more than 1 million Americans currently behind bars and better than three times that number on parole or probation, our country has the dubious honor of having the highest per capita imprisonment rate in the industrial world and is one of the only modern nations that still relies on capital punishment—hardly the record of a coddler.

And though politicians and citizens love to complain about violent offenders (like Willie Horton) released after having served only a fraction of their sentences, an article in the June [1994] *Atlantic Monthly* notes that "from 1975 to 1989 the average prison time served per violent crime tripled . . . and the prison population nearly tripled." Indeed, one of the key reasons why some violent offenders don't serve their full sentence is *not* the softness of our criminal-justice system but the fact that the 1980s' war on drugs and the accompanying strict mandatory-sentencing practices have glutted our prison system with drug offenders.

And what about all those middle- and upper-class Americans whose heightened concern about crime has gotten the attention of pollster and politician alike? Curiously enough, studies reported in both the *Economist* (October 15, 1994) and the *Wall Street Journal* (August 12, 1992) show not only that this is the population least threatened by violent crime but also that this group is actually safer today than it was two decades ago.

Indeed, numerous studies indicate that while stories of suburban wives carjacked by strangers capture the headlines and provoke moral and political outcries, the daily epidemic of violent crime in the U.S. actually tends to be concentrated in poor, inner-city neighborhoods and prefers victims that are young, poor, black, and male.

> *"The overall rate of crime in America has dropped over the past two decades."*

So while juveniles and blacks may commit a disproportionately large majority of violent crimes, they also constitute the largest group of its victims. In America, 16- to 19-year-olds are 20 times more likely than the elderly to be victims of violent crime, while homicide (taking the life of every 28th black male) is currently the leading cause of death among young black men. If crime has a war zone, it is not in the suburbs.

As to our "war on crime," although getting "tough" with criminals by building more prisons and imposing stiffer penalties appeals to voters, these approaches haven't reduced crime or made our streets safer. Since the early '80s we have nearly tripled our prison capacity and increased the Federal Bureau of Prison's budget over 470 percent, spending $21 to $24 billion a year on prison maintenance and construction. In the same period we have more than tripled our prison population by introducing increasingly stiffer penalties in the form of minimum mandatory sentences and different forms of Clinton's famous "three strikes" rule. And yet neither of these responses has had an appreciable effect on the rate of violent crime. Indeed, if anything, many studies indicated that instead of deterring future crimes, our increasingly massive prison system serves as a breeding ground for violent felons.

More Police Do Not Help Reduce Crime

All too often our inner-city youths experience imprisonment as both a rite of passage into manhood and a training school for more serious crimes. Thus, in neighborhoods where few youths could hope to go to community colleges or get decent jobs, our society ends up footing the bill for many of these young people to get a prison "education" with a tuition of $25,000 to $75,000 a year. Perhaps, then, it's not so surprising that some of the states with the highest rates in incarceration also have the worst statistics for violent crime. If stiffer sentences and more prisons are winning the "war on crime," it is certainly a Pyrrhic victory.

At the same time, while expanding our reliance on the death penalty or beefing up our police forces are popular political responses to crime, they are not effective ones. After decades of research, supporters of the death penalty have failed to produce any evidence that this punishment serves as a deterrent to violent crime or that its use makes our streets safer—in fact, recent data makes it clear that this approach is much more expensive to taxpayers than life in prison. Also, more than one expert has suggested that capital punishment is counterproductive because it helps to desensitize citizens to violence. This could be another reason

> *"Although getting 'tough' with criminals . . . appeals to voters, these approaches haven't reduced crime or made our streets safer."*

why so many civilized nations have abandoned its use and why numerous human-rights groups attack its continued employment in our country.

Further, while increasing police presence in some communities might be helpful, there are no studies justifying the call for a national buildup of our police force. Indeed, one landmark St. Louis study done in the '70s indicated that there was no correlation between a community's crime rate and the number of police assigned to it, while other research showed that although tripling the police presence in an area did increase the number of arrests, convictions, and imprisonments, it had little or no impact on the crime rate.

None of this is to say that police and prisons don't serve a valuable purpose. But these studies do indicate that a continuing shift away from the so-called soft approaches stressing education, employment, drug rehabilitation, and other forms of prevention is fatally flawed. While politicians were screaming at each other for cramming too much fat in the crime bill, the National Recreation and Park Association released a nationwide study proving that recreation and training programs could and did reduce the juvenile crime rate. Likewise, prevention programs involving outreach, education, and recreation cut the juvenile crime rates in Cincinnati, Dallas, and Fort Meyers between 24 and 27 percent.

Further, though an improving economy and decreasing unemployment figures gave middle- and upper-class voters the luxury to focus on crime and cry for tough penalties, things were different in America's poorest neighborhoods. There, even though people are much more likely to encounter violent crime, the hot issues—and the solutions to crime—continue to be the economy, unemployment, drugs, and education.

Perhaps that's because they know from experience that the crime that stalks their streets is not born simply of a malice we can contain with our police or break in our prisons but flows from a despair rooted in ignorance, poverty, addiction, and unemployment.

"Some of the states with the highest rates in incarceration also have the worst statistics for violent crime."

Study after study illustrates that crime in America is concentrated in the same neighborhoods having the worst schools, most devastating poverty, highest rates of unemployment, and worst problems of addiction. Unless we address these other issues, we can build prisons and hire police till we are blue in the face, but things won't get better.

Let me bring these reflections to a close by offering three thoughts for your consideration. First, it seems to me that any amount of crime, particularly violent crime, is too much, and that police and prisons are an important part of our response to this serious problem.

On the night my assailant attacked me, I was quite upset and frightened, and when three police cars responded to my 911 call and arrested my would-be mugger, I was genuinely relieved. Still—and this is my second point—I am convinced that our society's increasing and excessive reliance on punishment, as well as the public disdain we seem to have for prevention, is not just counterproductive but may say something unflattering about us as a community.

A Lack of Social Compassion

In the *Atlantic Monthly* article mentioned previously, author Wendy Kaminer suggests that the preference for punishment over prevention may reflect a darkly moralistic view of the world, devoid of hope either in prevention or rehabilitation. That view is very problematic for Christians. One who holds such a view lacks a basic compassion for those tempted to crime and wanders very near despair in failing to hope in people's capacity for repentance or conversion.

It's hard for me to see how such a view is compatible with our belief in a God who died to save us from our sins. Or perhaps—my final point—the preference for punishment is simply a form of apathy or sloth.

If we were to admit that crime was also a social problem, or that violent crime was an epidemic with multiple socioeconomic causes, then addressing it would demand complex, long-term, and costly solutions. Dealing with crime would involve caring about what happens to those in our worst neighborhoods and making a commitment to prevention, education, employment, and rehabilitation. That would take a lot of care and work.

In the end, I think we are confronted with two basic options in responding to crime. We may continue with "politics as usual" and, as Claude Raines suggests in *Casablanca*, "round up the usual suspects." Or we might follow the advice of Pope Paul VI, who suggested that "if you want peace, work for justice."

Let's remember those options the next time a politician promises to "get tough" on crime.

The Increasing Fear of Crime Is Unwarranted

by Rosellen Brown

About the author: *Rosellen Brown is the author of the novel* Before and After.

For many years, from the beginning of the 1970's, my family and I lived in Peterborough, a town of about 5,000 in southern New Hampshire. Thornton Wilder was in residence there when he wrote *Our Town*, which used, unchanged, the names of the nearest mountain and river and exemplified the community's peace, modesty and common sense.

A Crime-Free Small Town

Though we moved to Houston 13 years ago, we return to our old neighbors every summer, to the secure, nurturing society in which our children grew up. This is a town where shopkeepers still walk fearlessly down Main Street carrying their bags of cash- register money to the bank. Where a newspaper headline that read "Crack Found in High School" referred to the condition of its walls.

We continue to be devotees of the weekly newspaper, the *Peterborough Transcript*, which is mailed to our Houston home. Our favorite column has always been the "Police Log," which documents every call on its phone records and even reveals the ages of the recipients of traffic tickets.

Once, I remember, the log reported that someone had stolen a towel from the local motel. This chronicle continues to bring us word of barking and biting dogs, sick raccoons who wandered into civilization, a teenager who missed his curfew and scandals like the "funny odor" coming from an apartment that, after the evacuation of the building, turned out to be "somebody's bad cooking."

A few months ago, the log reported that the police had been summoned to witness a group playing a noisy game of Pictionary and warned them to proceed with less fervor. A week later, this item appeared: "Loud shouting, crying and other noises were reportedly heard at a Shadow Lane residence. Police found people watching football and asked them to quiet the noise." Possibly this was the same unruly group.

Of course the town's young people have discovered drugs. For adults in urgent need, Alcoholics Anonymous meets every night in an adjacent town. Physical and sexual abuse is gossiped about if not publicized. Relatively speaking, though, this place feels closer to Eden than to Sodom and Gomorrah.

Fear of Crime Erodes Small-Town Peace

But in the last year or two of reading the Police Log, we have noticed a turn to unwholesome imaginings by the citizens, who seem to have lost faith in their good fortune:

An unidentified man was seen sitting on a bench at Adams Playground. By the time the police came to investigate, he was gone.

The police received a report of a child in a van with two adults. The child was reportedly screaming, but when the police arrived they learned the child had been having a tantrum.

Someone came to a house reportedly selling children's encyclopedias. The books have not shown up yet.

A Central Street resident reported that someone in a white van called on her, trying to sell meat. When she said she wasn't interested, he pulled his card away abruptly and left.

If the Police Log can be seen as a portrait of the village psyche, it's clear that the interconnection of these townspeople, whose benign intentions were assumed as surely as the expectation that night would follow day, is endangered. Friendly neighbors once kept an eye on one another's kids and investigated possible problems themselves. Now, with a good deal less than provocation, they call the police. Often they don't leave their names.

> *"National statistics do not point to a hugely multiplying danger from lurking strangers in rural small towns."*

There is no evidence in these columns of any actual increase in abductions, molestations or rapes, or of a proliferation of con men preying on local residents. National statistics do not point to a hugely multiplying danger from lurking strangers in rural small towns.

This new wariness of strangers that we've found in recent Police Logs suggests that Our Town doesn't want to be left behind while a nation of victims nails up burglar protection bars and equips its children with Mace.

A rare horrific crime, like the [1993] abduction and murder of Polly Klaas in California or the [1993] kidnapping of Katie Beers in Long Island, carries far more potency today than the reality of 200 years of relative freedom from danger in a town where many people don't have keys to their front doors.

And since spring [1995] there has been a new nightmare to wake the sleepers in the Contoocook Valley, and it must be laid at the feet of those who detonated the peace of the so-called Heartland [bombing the Murrah Federal Building in Oklahoma City] on April 19 in the name of American values.

Chapter 2

Last month, the Police Log contained these two entries:

"A woman . . . said a man entered [an antique] shop and acted suspiciously. He reportedly took pictures down and examined the backs, then replaced them. The woman told police she was worried he might have planted a bomb. . . . Police investigated but found nothing unusual."

Then, after recounting some mischief concerning a BB gun and a petty robbery from a clothing store, the log continued:

> *"This unnatural terror, this poisoning of simple trust and calm, is a form of pollution . . . in the peaceful valleys of the nation."*

"A Pine Street resident reported seeing a large smoke cloud . . . on Vose Farm Road. Police found nothing, and theorize it was probably fog."

This unnatural terror, this poisoning of simple trust and calm, is a form of pollution that comes in under the door and seeps in around the windows in the peaceful valleys of the nation. When even the "safe" places are no longer perceived as exempt from the possibility of mayhem, they *are* no longer safe.

Chapter 3

Can Stronger Criminal Justice Measures Prevent Crime?

Chapter Preface

In October 1993, Polly Klaas, a twelve-year-old girl in Petaluma, California, was kidnapped and murdered by Richard Allen Davis, a man with a lengthy criminal record. Davis had been convicted and jailed three times for violent crimes before killing Klaas, and he had been released from prison only three months prior to the kidnapping. The case became the focal point for the campaign to adopt a "three strikes, you're out" law in California, mandating a life sentence for a criminal convicted of three violent felonies. Californians hoped that this new law would prevent future crimes like the murder of Polly Klaas.

Many conservatives support strict criminal justice measures, such as "three strikes" laws, as an effective way to prevent crime. Bruce Fein, a lawyer and freelance editorial writer, is among those who maintain that the majority of violent crimes are committed by a small minority of career criminals. Such felons commit repeated offenses, according to Fein, and are only stopped from doing so by being imprisoned. If such criminals were given lengthy sentences on their first violent felony, he reasons, they would be prevented from committing a host of further crimes. "Unforgiving prison terms for felons work to reduce crime," Fein concludes.

Many liberals, however, dispute whether harsh punishments can reduce crime rates. They point out that it is impossible to determine beforehand who is going to commit further crimes and who is going to be rehabilitated after a stay in prison. Bruce Shapiro, a contributing editor for the *Nation,* argues that it is unjust to impose lengthy prison terms on criminals simply because they might commit more crimes in the future. In his opinion, this is "nothing less than the end of the presumption of innocence."

A variety of strong criminal justice measures have been proposed and adopted throughout the United States as citizens seek to prevent heinous crimes like the murder of Polly Klaas. The viewpoints in the following chapter present contradictory opinions on the effectiveness of such measures in preventing violence and reducing crime rates.

Tougher Laws Can Prevent Crime

by William J. Bennett

About the author: *William J. Bennett is a fellow at the Heritage Foundation and the cochairman of the National Council on Crime in America, a bipartisan think tank.*

During the past 25 years, much of the crime debate has been dominated by criminologists who are philosophically opposed to punishment. In an attempt to advance their agenda, they have perpetrated a wide array of myths. The 1996 report of the bipartisan Council on Crime in America is an attempt to provide an alternative: a rigorous, empirical, real-world analysis of the current state of crime and punishment.

Steps to Preventing Crime

The report tells us that the nation faces at least three distinct but related crime challenges: preventing at-risk children from becoming criminals, protecting innocent people from becoming crime victims and restraining convicted criminals who are under the "supervision" of the criminal justice system (on probation, parole or pretrial release) from committing additional crimes.

• *Prevention.* We know that children born into poor families—no matter their race, region, religion, demographic stripe or socioeconomic status—if they have decent families and grow up with responsible, caring adults in their lives, are far less likely to become either victims or victimizers. We also know that not all children are born so lucky.

America is now home to nearly 70 million children 18 or under. As many as 15 million of them are growing up in relative poverty, often in places where the institutions of civil society—families, churches, schools, voluntary associations—are in near-complete collapse. The report argues that neither more spending by government nor the mere withdrawal of government can prevent today's at-risk 4- to 7-year-old boys from becoming the next decade's 14- to 17-year-old predatory street felons or the next century's first big class of adult

From William J. Bennett, "Shut the Criminals' Revolving Door," *Los Angeles Times,* editorial, January 16, 1996. Reprinted by permission of the author.

career criminals. The key to prevention is moral education. That, in turn, depends on reviving the character-forming institutions of civil society. But we know that there is no easy way to accomplish that.

• *Protection.* The recent widely reported drops in serious crime in New York, Houston and other cities were due largely to innovative community policing strategies, citizen anticrime initiatives and continued "target-hardening" or increased security and personal safety measures by individuals and businesses. But these drops in crime may be merely a lull. The storm is gathering in the form of a demographic bulge of highly crime-prone boys. During the next 10 years, enormous upward pressure will be exerted on crime rates. Redoubling crime protection efforts will not keep the storm offshore. But it can help to minimize the damage and reduce the human and financial cost.

• *Restraint.* The criminal justice system imprisons only one criminal per 100 violent crimes. Most violent prisoners serve less than half their time in prison before being released. In 1993, there were 43.6 million criminal victimizations in America, more than 10 million of them violent. Between 1985 and 1993, the rate at which boys 14 through 17 committed murder increased by about 50% for whites and 300% for blacks. A third of all violent crimes, including murders, are committed by felons out on probation, parole or pretrial release. What is involved here is more than a failure of public safety; it is a massive failure of governmental obligation.

> *"Citizens should not have to accept their government's prolonged, persistent failure to restrain violent and repeat criminals."*

Citizens should not have to accept their government's prolonged, persistent failure to restrain violent and repeat criminals. A government incapable of restraining known, violent, repeat criminals within its custody cannot be trusted to take on more complicated and costly public functions.

There is also the matter of eroding public trust in our political institutions. A government that, amid much fanfare, passes wave after wave of get-tough anti-crime laws but proves toothless in the execution of those laws eviscerates public confidence in the integrity of lawmakers and the criminal justice system. Indeed, in 1993 and again in 1994, there was only one public institution in which the American people had less confidence than in Congress: the criminal justice system. No representative democracy can long survive this deep and disheartening lack of public trust. And the only way to restore public trust is to shut the revolving door.

A final point: A society tells as much about itself by what it punishes as what it praises, by what it condemns as well as what it encourages, by what receives reprobation as what receives approbation. The message of our justice system is all too clear to criminals and victims: Too often, for too many, it says "nobody cares" and "nothing matters." That has to change soon or the carnage and violence that have become almost permanent features of America's landscape will worsen.

Imprisoning More Criminals Can Prevent Crime

by Steven D. Levitt

About the author: *Steven D. Levitt is a member of the Harvard Society of Fellows.*

Police and prisons represent the first line of defense in the fight against crime. In 1992 there were over 700,000 police officers in the United States (almost 50 percent more than two decades earlier), and over a million Americans in jails or prisons. The annual price tag for police and prisons is approaching $100 billion per year. In spite of all this, violent crimes per capita have risen 80 percent over the last two decades [since 1975].

Police and Prisons Can Reduce Crime

Does that mean our spending on police and prisons is a waste of money? Some observers have jumped to that conclusion, even going so far as to propose a moratorium on new prison construction. Research I have been conducting on the connection between police and prison availability and crime rates, however, comes to very different conclusions. Both police and prisons appear to be cost-effective tools in controlling crime, and each has been increasing in number simply because the underlying crime trend has been sharply upward. High crime rates make additional police necessary; that is why Detroit has twice as many police officers per capita as Omaha. The link between the size of the prison population and crime rates is even more direct: unless a justice system is growing more lenient, prison populations will rise one for one with crime rates.

The best practical way to judge the effectiveness of police and imprisonment is to study "natural experiments" where the number of police or prisoners fluctuate for reasons completely unrelated to crime incidence. By examining the effect of these changes in police or prisons on victimization levels, it is possible

From Steven D. Levitt, "Hiring Police and Building Prisons Pays Off," *American Enterprise,* May/June 1995. Reprinted by permission from the *American Enterprise,* a Washington, D.C.–based magazine of politics, business, and culture; Editor: (614) 375-2323.

to estimate causal impacts.

Mayoral and gubernatorial elections provide good ways to test the effectiveness of police reinforcements. In big cities, increases in police forces occur disproportionately during election years, presumably because incumbents want to look "tough on crime." Over the last two decades, police forces in cities with populations over 250,000 have grown an average of 2.8 percent in election years, but only 0.7 percent in non-election years.

After controlling election-induced changes in police staffing against other factors, one finds that police force expansions have large effects on crime rates. In the big cities I examined, an additional sworn officer eliminates 4.5 violent crimes and six property crimes each year. Based on the best estimates of costs of crime to victims, this reduction in crime is worth over $100,000 per officer per year. Any reduction in drunk driving, drug-related activities, arson, or fraud due to additional police would need to be added on top of that number, as would any psychological benefits to citizens from feeling safer. Given that the full costs of hiring a police officer are approximately $75,000 a year, it appears that hiring more police is a cost-effective approach to fighting crime in most cities.

The Costs of Prison vs. the Costs of Crime

Adding prisoners also appears to be a cost-beneficial strategy for reducing crime. The "natural experiment" I used in analyzing prisons grows out of prison overcrowding litigation brought by groups such as the American Civil Liberties Union. In many places, such suits have forced prison officials to release inmates. In states affected by such court orders, imprisonment levels lag the rest of the United States by an average of 15 percent over a three-year period. And during that time span, crime rates in those places rise 10 percent faster than the national average for violent offenses, and 5 percent faster for property crimes. I estimate that each additional prisoner taken off the streets eliminates between two and three violent crimes a year and over 10 property crimes. The economic benefits alone of preventing those crimes amount to approximately $45,000—well above annual incarceration costs that average $25,000 to $35,000 per prisoner.

> *"Both police and prisons appear to be cost-effective tools in controlling crime."*

How much crime might we reasonably hope to eliminate through increases in police and prisons? Putting another 100,000 police officers on the streets and an additional 100,000 offenders behind bars would likely reduce violent crime rates by about 10 percent. Beyond that point, diminishing returns make further increases economically unattractive.

"Three Strikes" Laws Can Prevent Crime

by Edwin Meese III

About the author: *Edwin Meese III, a former attorney general of the United States, is the Ronald Reagan Fellow in Public Policy at the Heritage Foundation.*

On Oct. 1, 1993, Polly Klaas was kidnapped at knifepoint from her Petaluma, Calif., home, where she had been enjoying a sleep-over with two teenage girl-friends. Subsequently she was found dead on a road about 45 miles from her house—strangled. The man identified in court documents as the killer had been convicted repeatedly of the most serious and dangerous crimes, including kidnapping, robbery, burglary and assault. Yet he was released from prison a few months before Polly's murder, serving only half of the 16-year sentence for his most recent felony.

High Profile Crimes by Repeat Offenders

More than a year earlier, Kimber Reynolds, an 18-year-old girl living in Fresno, Calif., was shot to death by a career criminal on parole, who killed her because she resisted his effort to steal her purse.

The nation was stunned in July 1993 by the fatal shooting of James Jordan, known as "Pops" to his basketball-star son, Michael Jordan. The elder Jordan's death occurred at a rest stop on Interstate 95 in North Carolina, at the hands of two men with long criminal histories of violent crimes.

These incidents that spanned the country, and hundreds of others taking place in the states in between, have triggered a massive reaction among law-abiding citizens. People are expressing their urgent fears about violent crime and demanding that new measures be taken to change the criminal justice system—particularly to protect against violent, repeat offenders who are being released into the community often after serving only a fraction of their sentences for previous crimes.

One of the measures most frequently proposed—perhaps because of its catchy title—is "three strikes and you're out," requiring that criminals involved

From Edwin Meese III, "Three-Strikes Laws Punish and Protect," *Insight* magazine, May 16, 1994. Reprinted with permission from *Insight.* Copyright 1994 by News World Communications, Inc. All rights reserved.

in three serious, violent felonies be sentenced to prison for guaranteed terms up to life imprisonment. The details of these proposals vary, but the essential concept is the same: Violent career criminals who have demonstrated their proclivity for repeated offenses should remain in prison for life or at least until the public can be absolutely assured that they no longer are a danger to society.

> *"Violent career criminals who have demonstrated their proclivity for repeated offenses should remain in prison for life."*

Despite extensive public approval—nearly 77 percent of Washington state voters launched a national movement for three-strikes laws by approving such a ballot initiative in October [1993]—a vigorous debate has been kindled among politicians, academics and criminal justice experts over the efficiency of such legislation. Dire warnings of overwhelming costs, potential "geriatric prisons" and misuse of limited resources are among the challenges posed by three-strikes opponents.

After a careful review of the arguments on both sides, I believe that laws providing guaranteed lengthy prison terms for violent career criminals, if properly written and applied, would materially increase public safety and improve our citizens' confidence in the criminal justice system.

An Effective Three-Strikes Law

First, however, let me suggest a few conditions that should govern such measures:

• A "three strikes and you're out" statute is not a panacea and will not solve all the problems that face our law enforcement and criminal justice institutions. This type of measure does not substitute for expanded and better-utilized police resources, reform of the juvenile justice system, better management of prisons, revision of criminal evidence laws or common-sense attention to the root causes of crime.

• Those drafting three-strikes legislation should remember the purpose of the concept: to keep repeat violent criminals out of circulation until they no longer are a danger to society. Therefore, it should apply to three violent offenses only (with the inclusion of home burglaries at night, since the crimes have such a high potential of violence), and not to just any three felonies.

• Since many violent criminals "burn out" in middle or advanced age, the term for three-time violent offenders should be near 25 years to life, with provisions for release of those who have served 25 or more years if correctional officials certify they no longer are dangerous.

• Three-strikes measures can be complementary to, and do not conflict with, other sentencing reforms that are under consideration, such as requiring violent criminals to complete 85 percent of the sentence meted out by the judge before they could be released from prison. Such a provision actually could result in fewer offenders becoming subject to three-strikes prerequisites: Well-structured sentences for early offenses, and an 85 percent serving requirement, reduce the opportunity for multiple-felony careers. The three-strikes law then serves as a "safety gate" to stop those offenders whose repeated criminality has not been ended by sound judicial sentences or appropriate lengths of imprisonment.

Three-Strikes Laws Target Career Criminals

The argument in favor of a three-strikes law is made on the basis of common sense and statistical research. Most criminal justice experts agree that career criminals, who represent a relatively small component of the offender population, commit a disproportionately high volume of violent crimes. The problem in effective sentencing and prison-release decisions is to determine which criminals likely are to be repeat offenders. Those who "qualify" for three-strike treatment are self-selected. By having a history wherein they have committed a violent felony, served their sentence, committed a second felony, completed a second sentence and now have committed the third violent felony, they have demonstrated that unless they are otherwise deterred they will continue this pattern of criminality. The three-strikes incarceration requirement provides a deterrent by incapacitating the criminal at least until advanced age permits a safe release.

Illinois Rep. Henry Hyde, a senior member of the House Judiciary Committee and a proponent of three-strikes legislation, summarizes the statistical argument well:

"Most violent crimes are committed by a relatively small number of career criminals. One good estimate is that just 7 percent of young men with lengthy arrest records commit two-thirds of all violent offenses. Eighty percent of those who commit three violent crimes will go on to commit a fourth. Most will receive absurdly light sentences. A murderer will spend seven years in jail, on average. A rapist, only four years.

"Keeping these irredeemable predators in prison for life—or at least for as many years as it takes to drain the criminality out of them—is the single-most effective step we can take to combat repeated violent crime. Not only will they be removed from their customary prey, but also their tough sentences will deter others from following in their footsteps."

> *"Career criminals, who represent a relatively small component of the offender population, commit a disproportionately high volume of violent crimes."*

In the state that pioneered the concept, the nation's first three-strikes law is working well—even changing the minds of some original opponents. John Carlson, president of the Seattle-based Washington Institute for Policy Studies, wrote that eight criminals who are facing the prospects of "striking out" under his state's new law include three sex offenders, all of whom have attempted murder, and one who committed murder; a four-time armed robber;

and four other career criminals who have accumulated between themselves 64 prior criminal convictions.

This demonstration of the law's effectiveness caused the Spokane *Spokesman-Review*—which originally had opposed three strikes—to "grudgingly admit the new law appears to be working." In the same editorial, that newspaper conceded that the new law was catching the two kinds of criminals it now targeted: "high-profile predators who rape or kill repeatedly; and offenders who terrorize the community with chronic strings of lesser but still serious crimes, such as robbery."

The criminal history of the first felon to be sentenced under Washington state's three-strikes statute demonstrates why this concept is necessary and cost-effective. In and out of prison most of his adult life, this 45-year-old criminal was convicted of kidnapping and robbery (at knifepoint), two offenses that constituted his fifth and sixth felony convictions. His earlier crimes involved auto theft, armed robbery, a bank holdup and robbing a mail carrier. He also had violated his parole on a separate occasion by stealing about $1,000 from an automated teller machine. By repeatedly committing these violent crimes—even while on parole—this felon showed that his propensity for criminality and endangering others would have resulted in a continuing series of offenses. The attendant costs would be the victims and the criminal justice system through the repeated need to arrest, prosecute and convict him. Beyond these offenses' massive monetary costs, the community's heightened fear of crime also must be recognized.

Refuting Arguments Against Three-Strikes Laws

Despite the extensive public appeal of three-strikes legislation, several reasons exist why someone would oppose it. The argument heard most often is that keeping people in prison for such a long time is too costly. But most responsible research into the cost-benefit ratio of imprisonment has shown that the actual cost of allowing a repeat criminal to roam free, continuing his depredation, is at least two to five times greater than the expense of keeping him in prison. This is particularly true of violent criminals; the savings in terms of human suffering must be added to a cost comparison.

Another argument voiced against long, mandatory sentences for career criminals is that this will create "geriatric prisons" and that taxpayers will be forced to pay the high cost of health care and other expenses for elderly prisoners whose age prevents them from being a continuing danger to society. However, well-drafted

> *"The actual cost of allowing a repeat criminal to roam free . . . is at least two to five times greater than the expense of keeping him in prison."*

statutes should permit the release of such inmates when they have completed a minimum period (generally, 25 years) and the appropriate judicial or correctional officials are convinced they no longer are dangerous.

Opponents of three-strikes laws also claim that such measures take away discretion from the judge who is charged with the task of sentencing the career criminal. While this is true, the popularity of the law with the public reflects dissatisfaction with the sentencing and correctional practices that have returned violent offenders to the community too rapidly and have enabled them to continue their harmful ways. The three-strikes law does not interfere with judicial discretion during the early phases of a criminal's history, but does provide a mandatory stopping point when all other means of deterring a violent, repeat offender have failed.

Punish the First Two Strikes as Well

Curiously, some have opposed the three-strikes rule as being too weak. "Why," they ask, "should a criminal be allowed to harm his victims as many as three times? Why not give him a long prison term on the first offense or at least the second serious offense?" Such long terms may be appropriate and usually are available by statute prior to the third conviction. There is nothing in the three-strikes concept that prevents severe punishment when it is deserved at an earlier stage. What the three-strikes law provides is a final barrier that keeps a confirmed criminal separated from society until he or she is no longer a menace.

> "[Efforts to address the causes of crime] are not incompatible with strong, immediate measures to cope with the present danger of career criminals."

Perhaps the most serious issue concerning the three-strikes rule has been advanced by author and conservative writer William Tucker in the *American Spectator*. Tucker postulates that more career criminals—those with two or more convictions who would qualify for life imprisonment on their next offense—are likely to kill their victims to avoid future identification, since the penalty for murder is no greater than the life term they already face.

While there is no available evidence that such a situation has commonly occurred in the 35 states that have other forms of habitual-offender laws, it is a concern that must be addressed. Most proponents of three-strikes laws believe that the possible risk of some career criminals killing witnesses or pursuing police officers because "they have nothing to lose" is more than outweighed by the benefit of permanently denying large numbers of violent, repeat offenders the opportunity to continue their dangerous crimes.

They argue that the chance of an "ordinary" robbery escalating into murder is greater than the probability of a witness being killed deliberately. Also, an enhanced penalty still would exist for those who kill during an otherwise nonfatal offense since such murderers would have no chance for parole, while career criminals who do not kill would have the hope of release at some point when they no longer are considered dangerous.

But Tucker actually provides the answer to this dilemma in his article, which is less an argument against the three-strikes law than it is a compelling argument for an effective death penalty.

To prevent the murder of witnesses and police officers at the hands of dangerous criminals who seek to avoid arrest—which occurs today even without the three-strikes law—society needs the ultimate penalty of capital punishment.

Immediate Action Is Needed

Finally, some argue that instead of lock-'em-up strategies such as three-strikes requirements, we should give more attention and resources to dealing with the root causes of crime. Efforts to realistically deal with the underlying conditions that contribute to criminality should be encouraged, including changes in welfare-state programs and other public policies that exacerbate the problems of most low-income communities. But such long-term initiatives are not incompatible with strong, immediate measures to cope with the present danger of career criminals.

When a fire is raging in a community, prudence requires immediate action to put it out rather than devoting total effort and resources toward a future-oriented fire-prevention scheme.

Hyde emphasizes this priority well when he summarizes the reasons the public strongly supports three-strikes-and-you're-out rules for violent offenders in state and federal jurisdictions: "Sociologists can ponder and research the root cause of crime all they want (and for as long as their grant money holds out). But a three-time violent criminal needs to be removed from society—permanently. It's as simple as that. And the American people know it, even if their courts, parole boards and legislatures have been slow to catch on."

Community Policing Strategies Can Prevent Crime

by **Richard Cohen**

About the author: *Richard Cohen is a columnist for the* Washington Post.

The car was parked on East 84th, near the intersection with Park Avenue, and in the window was a sign that said, "No Radio." At one time, such signs were common here—"No Radio," "No Nothing," "Everything Stolen"—but it had been a long time since I'd seen one. I crossed the street to get a better look. Ah, Virginia tags. I guess they hadn't heard.

A Dramatic Decline in Crime

But how could they not? A wonderful thing has happened to New York. It has rolled back the years. In terms of murder, it's 1968—the year I left for Washington—but it feels like the 1950s, which is about as far back as I remember, when crime was an inconvenience, like the weather, and not a mortal threat that circumscribed your life. New York was never all that safe—this is Gotham City, after all—but rarely has it been as dangerous as it recently was.

The change has been dramatic, virtually miraculous and—to be perfectly honest—a bit inexplicable. The mayor, Rudolph Giuliani, is a former prosecutor who just hates the bad guys. He appointed a police commissioner, William Bratton, who started to make "quality of life" arrests. No drinking on the streets—that sort of thing. Earlier, as the chief of the transit police, Bratton had arrested fare jumpers and learned something amazing: A large number of them were armed. Arrest them for jumping a subway turnstile and you get them before they commit an armed robbery.

Bratton is the police commish no more, but the cops still practice what he preached, and crime remains amazingly low. Lots of people, especially the police, credit the police—and maybe they are right. Others point to dumb luck, trends in drug trafficking (fewer turf wars) and demographics—a dip in the number of young men in the population.

Young men commit most of the crime, and much of their crime is violent. The numbers of young men will soon be starting on the way up, and in the view of some criminologists we ain't seen nothing yet. These kids are heartless beasts—gun-toting and remorseless. John J. DiIulio Jr. of Princeton's Center for Public Management has given them a name: "Superpredator." In such creative ways are academic reputations made.

Still, demographics can't explain everything. Crime is down almost uniformly and even Washington, D.C., in a virtually inexplicable improvement, experienced a dip in its murder total in 1995—and then, because it is traditional, the number of murders resumed its march upward. But the New York figures are so startling—the number of murders dropped by half over the past five years and, most significant, murder by strangers (19 percent of all homicides) is way down—that something other than demographics must be at work.

Police Prevent Crime

Until we are told otherwise, we can only conclude that the cops made a difference. In some respects, this runs counter to the conventional wisdom—the belief in certain circles that cops could be pretty good at catching criminals but were powerless to stop crime before it happened. This was the consensus in many scholarly journals and, as usual, there were studies to back up the thesis: Cops really don't matter all that much.

> *"We can only conclude that the cops made a difference [in the crime rate]."*

Now it seems otherwise. Bust someone for jumping a turnstile or drinking in the street and, most important, take his gun away and you're likely to get him before he commits a more serious crime. Do that often enough and criminals stop carrying guns.

But in addition to sending a message to criminals, such tactics send a message to ordinary citizens as well. Once again, they feel that the rules of society apply to all of us—that you can't spit on the street, put your feet up on the subway seats, play your radio too loud, get drunk in public or, even, make a nuisance of yourself by lunging into traffic to "clean" the windshields of cars that do not need it anyway.

For a frequent visitor such as myself, the change in New York is not limited just to statistics. You can sense it on the street—those vanished "No Radio" signs, for instance, and the absence of car alarms going off in the night. People are no longer admonished not to walk here or go there. And unless something happened on New Year's Eve, Central Park, where that poor jogger was gang raped and nearly bludgeoned to death in 1989, has gone the year [1996] without a single homicide. The city has made the most wonderful sort of progress—backward to a better time.

Where have you gone, Joe DiMaggio?

Tougher Laws Will Not Prevent Crime

by Malcolm C. Young and Marc Mauer

About the authors: *Malcolm C. Young is the executive director and Marc Mauer is the assistant director of the Sentencing Project in Washington, D.C.*

"Law and order" politicians and ideologues have long contended that the way to defeat violent crime is to lock up more people in prison for longer terms. The latest salvo in the conservative attack is a January 1996 report from the newly-formed Council on Crime in America, co-chaired by Griffin Bell and William Bennett. The Council describes itself as an organization that "seeks to provide rigorous, factual information" and portrays its report, *The State of Violent Crime in America*, by Council member John DiIulio, as a comprehensive analysis of the problem.

Correcting Myths About Crime and Imprisonment

In fact, the report actually misrepresents the realities of crime and punishment through a highly selective and, at times, deceptive use of government data. Following are some examples taken from the report's heavily publicized "Ten Highlights":

"More than half of convicted violent felons are not even sentenced to prison." Wrong. The Council's own numbers demonstrate that *more than half* of violent felons go to prison. Bureau of Justice Statistics data for 1992 (the most recent year for which data are available) put the number at 60 percent, with an additional 21 percent sentenced to jail terms. In total, four out of five people convicted of violent offenses end up behind bars. Those who do not tend to be those convicted of less serious assaults.

"One out of four criminal victimizations in America today is violent." True, but misleading. Nearly half of the 10.9 million violent crimes annually are simple assaults without injury, such as barroom brawls or schoolyard fights—not the murders, rapes, and robberies that are of more serious concern.

"The justice system imprisons barely one criminal for every 100 violent

From Malcolm C. Young and Marc Mauer, "Lie: Harsher Sentences Make Us Safer." This article was reprinted from *Covert Action Quarterly,* Summer 1996, 1500 Massachusetts Ave. NW, #732, Washington, DC 20005; phone: (202) 331-9763; e-mail: caq@igc.apc.org. Annual subscriptions payable by check, money order, or credit card (VISA/MasterCard): U.S. $22; Canada $27; Europe $33.

crimes." True, but again misleading, as the Council well knows. Half of all violent crimes are never even reported, fewer than half of those reported result in an arrest, and ultimately, only about 2 percent of violent crimes result in a conviction. As noted above, most of those convicted are imprisoned. This statistic also inadvertently points out a serious problem with the Council's approach: The criminal justice system is reactive; it comes into play after the harm has been done. Preventing violence in the first place must be an equally important objective.

"*Since 1974, over 90 percent of all state prisoners have been violent offenders or recidivists.*" This statement is a serious distortion because it lumps together Charles Manson (violent) with a check forger who was once convicted of juvenile joyriding (recidivist). Overall, 38 percent of prison inmates have never been convicted of a violent offense, and more than half are nonviolent property or drug offenders. Further, in the last decade [since 1986], the proportion of violent offenders in prison has been declining because of a surge in people imprisoned for drug offenses.

Crowding Prisons with Drug Offenders

"*The average quantity of drugs involved in federal cocaine trafficking cases is 183 pounds.*" A first semester statistics student would know that a few major drug smugglers importing drugs by the planeload will greatly distort the "average" quantity of drugs involved in overall drug trafficking cases. In fact, Justice Department data show that the median amount of drugs seized in cocaine trafficking arrests was less than four pounds—roughly 2 percent of the 183-pound figure the Council touts. A 1994 Justice Department report concluded that one-third of federal drug offenders were "low-level" offenders. The number is further skewed because federal prosecutors generally choose to prosecute the higher-level drug offenses and leave lower-level offenses for state prosecutors. People imprisoned for drug offenses at the state level are thus likely to include large numbers of low-level offenders as well.

> "*The criminal justice system is reactive. . . . Preventing violence in the first place must be an equally important objective.*"

"*Most violent prisoners serve less than half their time in prison before being released.*" Members of the Council, all of whom have extensive criminal justice experience, know that judges impose sentences based on a calculation of how much time a person will serve. If a given state releases most inmates at half their maximum sentence, then judges will impose a ten-year sentence if they think the inmate should serve five years. There is nothing deceptive about this. In fact, the possibility of gaining early release on parole has long been recognized as the most important reward that prison wardens can hold out for good behavior.

Perhaps the most disingenuous aspect of this report, and the conservative barrage in general, is its failure to acknowledge that those making the everyday decisions about community safety are judges, prosecutors, parole officials, and other criminal justice professionals—groups which could hardly be regarded as "soft on crime" except by ax-grinding demagogues.

Criminal justice policy should be based on accurate data and analysis, not misrepresentative displays of data. Unfortunately, that is just what the Council on Crime in America relies on.

Rehabilitating Criminals Can Prevent Crime

by Charles W. Colson

About the author: *Charles W. Colson is the founder of Prison Fellowship, a religious ministry for prison inmates.*

As the House and Senate prepare to vote on the final version of the $33 billion crime bill [the 1994 Omnibus Crime Act], the nation's attention is rightly riveted on a crime crisis that has grown to alarming proportions. Yet in today's frenzy to fight crime, no one consults the real experts: the criminals themselves.

Criminals Reveal How to Prevent Crime

Prison Fellowship, an organization I helped found after serving time for Watergate-related offenses, decided to do just that. In our newspaper, *Inside Journal* distributed free to prisoners nationwide, we invited inmates to write to us, answering the question, "What could have stopped you from breaking the law?"

Nearly 600 prisoners responded. Their letters are snapshots of families fractured by violence, of childhoods spent "not listening to anyone." The inmates agonize over drug and alcohol addiction; they rage at years wasted behind bars. A number of the letters flicker with hopes and dreams—the urge to reunite with their wives and children, to rebuild their lives. Most of all, they gave honest answers to the factors that led to crime.

Here are the tips we gleaned from the inmates:

1) *We can fight crime by building community ties.* A prisoner in Maine wrote, "My main job was breaking and entering. What I've noticed most about the houses I have hit is that none of my victims lived in a crime watch district."

The lesson is that community awareness programs do work. Programs such as Neighborhood Watch and National Night Out are effective vehicles for teaching citizens how to protect their homes, pass on safety skills to children and work cooperatively with local police departments.

Preventing crime is everybody's job. Community-based programs are the most widely tested and proven antidote to crime, not to mention the most cost-effective. The National Crime Prevention Council notes, in its *Organizers' Handbook*, that law enforcement agencies nationwide "report substantial decreases in crime due to citizens' self-help education and preventive efforts."

2) *We can fight crime by opposing media violence.* An Alabama inmate, in prison for robbery, wrote: "Watching TV and seeing people do robberies—and the way it has been glamorized on TV—made me think of doing it myself."

Psychologists debate endlessly over whether television violence causes crime. But inmates themselves tell us without hesitation that much of their inspiration comes from TV. Many shows are so detailed and graphic that they are virtually how-to manuals in crime. According to surveys reported in the *Journal of the American Medical Association*, as many as one-third of young male prisoners convicted of violent crime say they were consciously imitating techniques they learned from television.

3) *We can fight crime by building healthy families.* One of the most poignant letters came from a Michigan prisoner: "I was told all the time I was growing up that I was no-good and would never amount to anything. I was beaten . . . almost every day of the week. I wasn't allowed to have any friends come over."

Overwhelming numbers of prisoners report growing up in homes where indifference or terror or both reigned. Sex offenders are particularly likely to say they were abused as youngsters, threatened with death if they told anyone.

There is no question that many maltreated kids grow into dangerous adults. The National Institute of Justice found that childhood abuse increases the odds of future criminality by 40%. The first line of defense against crime is to build strong and healthy families.

Programs to Rehabilitate Criminals Prevent Crime

4) *We can fight crime by helping criminals.* In today's political climate, the emphasis is on convicting criminals and locking them up—not on what happens to them inside. But 97% of those who go in eventually come back out. What kind of people will they be then?

The answer is chilling: Many immediately fall back into a life of crime. One prisoner wrote of the irony of expecting prison to curb violent behavior. "Prison—where violence and drugs are an everyday occurrence," he wrote. "Prison—where men speak of all the money, women and drugs they've had from stealing." When they come out, most inmates are simply schooled in more sophisticated methods of committing crime.

> *"The first line of defense against crime is to build strong and healthy families."*

If we want them to be schooled in something more productive, it's imperative that we provide educational and vocational programs. Nationally, the rate of inmates who are rearrested after release is 60% to 70%. But among inmates who receive two years of education, the rate drops to a mere 10%. Perhaps it's time to require inmates to participate in educational, literacy, vocational and substance abuse programs.

5) *We can fight crime by encouraging moral behavior.* Ultimately, I believe the solution to our crime problem is a spiritual one. Prison Fellowship organizes volunteers to run Bible studies and seminars behind bars. We challenge inmates to tap into the most potent force available for reforming their lives: the power of Jesus Christ. Across the country, 55,000 Prison Fellowship volunteers are involved in all aspects of working with inmates, their families and victims of crime.

We also run marriage seminars for inmates. Of prisoners who are married, 85% see their marriages fail. Most of the rest split up within a year after the spouse is released. Yet studies show that the most important factor in setting a criminal straight is responsibility for a family. Our marriage seminars help inmates reconcile with their spouses and learn Biblical principles of forgiveness and trust.

> *"Ultimately, I believe the solution to our crime problem is a spiritual one."*

Our Life Plan seminars are aimed at prisoners about to be released. The seminars teach them how to set realistic goals for getting a job, finding a place to live, joining a church and building a support network. When prisoners are released, Life Plan matches each one with a volunteer mentor, who is often an ex-convict himself. The mentor offers support during the first six months in the outside world—the time when the risk is highest for falling back into crime.

If America wants to get tough on crime, this is the way to do it. Offering programs to prisoners does not mean "coddling" them; it means challenging them to change from the inside, to accept responsibility for their lives and their families.

"Three Strikes" Laws Will Not Prevent Crime

by Ethan Fletcher and Nick Turner

About the authors: *Ethan Fletcher and Nick Turner are former interns at* Dollars and Sense, *a bimonthly magazine of left perspectives on current economic affairs.*

Washington State's Persistent Offender Accountability Act (Initiative 593) provided the country with its first look at the future of American criminal justice. Passed in November 1993 by 76% of the voters, the well-known "Three Strikes and You're Out" provision mandates life imprisonment without parole for those convicted of a serious offense for the third time. Since then, California and New Mexico have passed similar ordinances, and 30 other states are considering Three Strikes legislation. The passage of Clinton's anticrime bill [the 1994 Omnibus Crime Act] puts this policy in place for federal crimes.

Three Strikes Is a Popular Response to Crime

Recent polls have indicated that as much as 80% of the public supports some form of Three Strikes. Republican and Democratic politicians from across the nation are appeasing their crime-weary constituents by promising to make Three Strikes law in their states. New York's Democratic Governor Mario Cuomo is supporting the bill in part to compensate for his unpopular opposition to the death penalty. In California, Republican Governor Pete Wilson's speeches evoked the Polly Klaas case (12-year-old Klaas was kidnapped and murdered [in 1993] by a repeat offender) to drum up support for the initiative. Some overzealous legislators have cried to one-up their competition, calling for "Two Strikes and You're Out" laws, and even "Three Strikes and You're Dead."

On the surface, Federal Bureau of Investigation (FBI) statistics provide a rationale for Three Strikes. The FBI says that 6% of criminals commit about 70% of all crimes. By one theory, if it were possible to lock up this relatively small group of criminals for life, there would be a noticeable spike in public safety.

Critics of Three Strikes, like the American Civil Liberties Union (ACLU), argue that despite its all-American slogan, the legislation is not in the country's

From Ethan Fletcher and Nick Turner, "Three Strikes and We're All Out," *Dollars and Sense,* November/December 1994. Reprinted with permission. *Dollars and Sense* is a progressive economics magazine published six times a year. First-year subscriptions cost $18.95 and may be ordered by writing to *Dollars and Sense,* One Summer Street, Somerville, MA 02143.

interest. The ACLU has outlined many of its drawbacks, including the elimination of judicial discretion in sentencing and the disproportionate impact the policy will have on people of color.

Critics have made a solid case that Three Strikes will cost taxpayers billions of dollars, but won't increase our safety. They point out that half of felonies are committed by people aged 20 to 29, while only one 1% of serious offenses are committed by those over the age of 60. According to the ACLU, keeping a younger convict in prison costs about $25,000 per year, while imprisoning an older person requires $60,000 per year due to health bills and other expenses. This means that if the 70 offenders who will qualify for Initiative 593 in 1994 live to be 80, the cost to taxpayers to house them from age 60 until death will be $84,000,000, and the public safety benefits will be negligible.

> *"Critics have made a solid case that Three Strikes will cost taxpayers billions of dollars, but won't increase our safety."*

The ACLU has described Three Strikes as "a misguided plan that will amount to geriatrics in jail, while not increasing safety." Doug Honig, the Public Education Director of the ACLU's Washington branch, explained further that funds spent to house inmates and build more prison space will be unavailable to fight crime in other ways, and public safety, therefore, may actually suffer as a result of Three Strikes.

Another problem, identified by a team of representatives from the Washington Association of Churches, the Washington State Catholic Conference, the ACLU of Washington, and the Washington Association of Criminal Defense Lawyers, is the broad definition of a serious offense. Under the law, two third-time offenders, one who commits a brutal murder and another who steals $100 while using a weapon, could receive identical automatic sentences of life without parole in prison.

One of the most stinging examples of this problem is the case of Larry Fisher. Fisher became one of Washington State's first candidates for Initiative 593 when he was arrested in January 1994 for robbing a sandwich shop of $151. Fisher, who was sentenced to life in prison in April, hardly embodies the ruthless criminal element that Americans fear. His second and third strikes came from two robberies where he used a concealed finger as a "gun."

Three Strikes Laws May Increase Violence

Three Strikes will cause other harm besides unnecessarily sentencing criminals to life in prison. As corrections officer Dave Paul explained in a March 1994 edition of the *Portland Oregonian*, criminals with two prior "most serious offense" convictions will do anything to avoid a third. If apprehended committing a lesser "most serious offense" such as robbery or assault, the felon has nothing to lose by resisting arrest. Paul warns that we should "expect assaults on police and correctional officers to rise precipitously." Costs will also rise. As

Paul asks, if a two-time offender is arrested, "Is he going to plead guilty and go to prison for life or take the chance a jury will find him not guilty, or that an error by a prosecutor will allow him to go free? He's going to take a jury trial, with all the added expenses."

Furthermore, while the public is demanding an end to violent crime now, simple logic dictates that Three Strikes laws will have virtually no impact for about ten years, the period that a three-time serious offender would typically serve under the current laws of most states. Since the new laws apply only to people being convicted in the future, not to existing inmates, the new convicts would not be released for a decade anyway. So the crime-fighting benefits of this new legislation cannot be known until then.

Whether or not public safety improves, states implementing Three Strikes would feel an economic crunch the eleventh year. In states like New York and California, hundreds of Three Strikes candidates will be arrested each year. As more offenders are locked up for life, the costs will explode.

Three Strikes is really just a tougher version of the habitual offender laws and recidivist statutes that were implemented years ago. Seventeen states already dole out harsher sentences for repeat offenders. "None of these laws have had much of an impact on crime," the ACLU argues. "The government may be justified in punishing a repeat offender more severely than a first offender, but Three Strikes laws are overkill."

Florida, for example, instituted its habitual criminal law in the late 1980s. Repeat offenders are required to serve 70% to 80% of their term, compared with 19% for other criminals. This law has had little impact. In the years since it was implemented, the violent crime rate in Florida, already the worst in the nation, increased by 16%. In 1994, Florida legislators rejected a Three Strikes proposal, calling it too costly.

> *"Three Strikes will cause other harm besides unnecessarily sentencing criminals to life in prison."*

The habitual offender laws at the federal level were also more than adequate and did not need to be beefed up by Clinton's crime bill. Federal courts already hand out near-maximum sentences for career criminals. Furthermore, the federal version of Three Strikes applies only to those criminals whose third strike constitutes a federal offense.

Alternative Measures to Prevent Crime

If federal and state governments are determined to increase their crime-fighting efforts, there are several less expensive and more productive steps they could take:

• A drive to limit the availability of firearms is in order. Thankfully, the federal crime bill addressed this topic, with its ban on some assault weapons. Violent crimes are easier to commit when deadly weapons are readily available.

• Drug treatment centers should be improved and expanded. The majority of

criminals charged with robbery or burglary test positive for drug use. Nevertheless, rehabilitation is not an option for many Americans because treatment centers are overwhelmed by applicants, and thousands are put on waiting lists. Increased funding would insure that more drug users receive the help they need.
Judges should also include treatment as part of the sentences for drug-addicted
criminals.

• Courts should be given the freedom to impose creative sentences when dealing with non-violent offenders. Alternative sentencing programs, which are
growing in popularity across the nation, allow courts to hand down punishments that suit the crimes. For the most part, alternative sentencing consists of
community service, or a punishment that would be especially meaningful to the
offender. For example, a Memphis judge allowed the victims of a burglar to
come to the perpetrator's house and take anything they wanted. Such programs
save money and can free up jail space for the truly dangerous criminals.

Community Policing Is an Alternative

• Community policing is another option that federal and state governments
should consider. It is not enough that Clinton's crime package provides funding
for 100,000 more police. The effectiveness of these men and women in fighting
crime will be determined by *how* they police. Community policing is an effective way to address crime, not only when it happens, but before it happens. Police should know their neighborhoods and defuse potentially violent situations. States would

> *"As more offenders are locked up for life, the costs will explode."*

also be wise to employ more probation officers. Criminals on probation will be
less likely to commit more crimes if they are being monitored carefully. Currently, probation officers are swamped with cases (some have more than 100)
and cannot supervise them all effectively. An infusion of funding could ease
their burdens.

None of these suggestions have catchy slogans like Three Strikes, and few of
them would strike a chord with the American public, but they all would be effective crime-fighting measures. Furthermore, they would cost billions less than
simply locking up criminals for life. Voters and politicians must look beyond
quick-fix proposals, and examine the roots of crime. Until then, no amount of
money will cure America's epidemic of violence.

Community Policing Strategies Do Little to Prevent Crime

by Richard Moran

About the author: *Richard Moran is a professor of sociology and criminology at Mount Holyoke College in South Hadley, Massachusetts.*

New York Mayor Rudolph Giuliani and his former police commissioner, William Bratton, have seized credit for the abrupt drop in New York City's murder rate. They claim that their policing strategy of "zero tolerance" for minor lawbreakers like squeegee men has made New York safe again; now other cities, including Washington, D.C., are heralding their tactics as the best way to combat crime.

No Correlation Between Police and Declining Murder Rates

But while the argument that the police deserve all the credit for the drop in homicides sounds plausible, no solid scientific evidence supports their claims of omnipotence. Indeed, the weight of the evidence suggests that the mayor and his commissioner were simply in the right place at the right time.

The most significant thing one needs to know about the annual homicide rate is that it fluctuates. Look at the figures for New York City over the past 20 years, and you'll find that the homicide rate has twice gone down and twice gone up. From 1981 to 1985, murder fell by 24 percent (from 1,832 to 1,392), and from 1991 to 1996 murders declined by 55 percent (from 2,161 to 984). On the other hand, from 1978 to 1981, murders jumped 21 percent (from 1,518 to 1,832), and from 1985 to 1990 they soared 63 percent (from 1,392 to 2,262). Like the decline in snowfall in New England this winter [1997] after years of unusually high amounts, homicides in New York City also have returned to more normal levels.

The "broken windows" theory is a cornerstone of New York's policing strat-

From Richard Moran, "The New York Story: More Luck Than Policing," *Washington Post National Weekly Edition*, February 17-23, 1997. Reprinted by permission of the author.

egy. It purports to explain how disorder, incivility and urban decay lead to crime: If a window is broken and remains unfixed, before long more windows will be broken. Because such transgressions proclaim that no one is in charge, official tolerance for nuisances such as graffiti and panhandling hastens a neighborhood's decline and animates serious crime. Aggressive enforcement of minor legal violations is the presumed remedy. By fixing broken windows, and arresting window breakers, the theory goes, a city sends criminals the message that law-abiding citizens retain control of the streets.

Testing the Broken Windows Hypothesis

The contention that "grime leads to crime by attracting slime" is a seductive hypothesis. The empirical support for it, however, is weak. Improving a neighborhood's economic profile is at least as important. Ralph Taylor of Temple University has conducted one of the most extensive studies of the "grime, slime, crime" hypothesis. For 30 neighborhoods in Baltimore, he analyzed three decades of crime and census information, conducted on-site assessments of neighborhood deterioration in 1981 and 1994, interviewed residents in 1982 and 1994 and talked to community leaders in 1994. In short, he explored the ability of natural variations in neighborhood deterioration to predict changes in crime. After accounting for a neighborhood's socioeconomic standing, racial makeup and community stability, he found that deterioration did result in some changes in subsequent crime rates.

> *"While the argument that the police deserve all the credit for the drop in homicides sounds plausible, no solid scientific evidence supports their claims."*

But his principal conclusion remains: Crime leads to grime more than vice versa.

In truth, what New York City provides is an interesting but essentially unprovable correlation between police practices and declining homicide rates. Unfortunately, the city's new policing strategies were implemented in a way that makes it impossible to evaluate their supposed effectiveness on the violent crime and homicide rate. If they had been introduced in some precincts and not in others, or if they had been part of a carefully controlled scientific experiment, then it might have been possible to evaluate the strategies scientifically.

A close and careful look at the data, however, reveals one indisputable fact that cannot be reconciled with the argument that the change in police methods is solely responsible. The decline in the murder rate began in 1991, three years before Giuliani and Bratton took office. Although the decline did accelerate shortly after they took office, this was only to be expected. All trends take a while to gain momentum, whether we are talking about economic recovery, global warming or homicide rates.

And although New York City experienced the most dramatic decline, murder and violent crime have declined nationwide. Some cities that experienced a drop in crime adopted new policing practices, but many did not. For instance, East St. Louis, Ill., one of the most economically depressed cities in America, experienced a 60 percent decline in the homicide rate over the same period, from 67 homicides in 1991 to 27 homicides in 1996. During this time no new police practices were introduced. Rather, East St. Louis was so deep in debt that police layoffs were common. Most police cars did not have functioning two-way radios, and many remained idle due to the lack of money for gas. Nonetheless, proportionately the homicide rate declined more dramatically in East St. Louis than it did in New York City.

Police Do Not Prevent Crime

Not surprisingly, experienced criminologists have been reluctant to endorse the claims of Giuliani and Bratton. Over 30 years of criminological research has shown that the ability of the police to influence crime is extremely limited.

For example, neither the number of police in a community nor the style of policing appears directly related to the crime rate. In 1991, San Diego and Dallas had about the same ratio of police to population, yet twice as many crimes were reported in Dallas. Meanwhile, Cleveland and San Diego had comparable crime rates even though Cleveland had twice as many police officers per capita. And in 1992, the District of Columbia had both the highest homicide rate and the most metropolitan police per square foot of any city in the nation.

If more police do not mean less crime, what about foot patrols? After all, they are another one of the cornerstones of the new policing strategy. The most thorough study ever done, a 1981 analysis of police beats in Newark, N.J., found that foot patrols had virtually no effect on crime rates. Cops walking the beat did make people, especially shopkeepers, feel safer, but they did not lower the crime rate.

> *"The contention that 'grime leads to crime by attracting slime' is a seductive hypothesis. The empirical support for it, however, is weak."*

Even if a foot patrol officer manages to restore a small measure of order and civility to the urban landscape, the officer remains powerless to affect the social and economic forces that shape the lives of people in the inner cities. Poverty, lack of education, addiction and the paucity of jobs for unskilled workers are the real causes of crime and neighborhood deterioration.

Most seasoned criminologists have a more plausible explanation for the decline in murder in New York City. They point to a twofold increase in the number of criminals sent to jail over the past 10 years, an improving economy that has summoned idle young men back to full time work and, most importantly, the waning of the murderous crack wars as the most likely reasons murder has declined there and elsewhere. New York was among the first cities in which crack appeared, and it is the place where its decline has been the most dramatic.

The drug trade arrived in smaller cities one to five years later, which helps explain why New York has led the decline in big city murders. It also bodes well for the future of homicide rates nationwide, especially in smaller cities.

Cleaning Up New York City

To give them their due, Mayor Giuliani and former police commissioner Bratton have restored a measure of civility and order to city streets. Tourists and citizens are less likely to be hassled by aggressive panhandlers, and less likely to have to confront the savage inequalities of modern urban life by being forced to step around or over the vagrants who once inhabited the city's public places. And their belligerent stop-and-frisk policy has taken guns out of the hands of some unsavory characters.

> *"Over 30 years of criminological research has shown that the ability of the police to influence crime is extremely limited."*

Their most noteworthy achievement, however, may be one they don't boast about: Their ability to convince New Yorkers and even many civil libertarians that rounding up "slime-balls" is a justifiable way to make life more agreeable for the honest, hard-working and socially acceptable people of New York, whether or not it actually reduces serious crime.

Chapter 4

How Can Juvenile Crime Be Prevented?

Preventing Juvenile Crime: An Overview

by Jean Hellwege

About the author: *Jean Hellwege is senior editor of* Trial, *the monthly magazine of the Association of Trial Lawyers of America.*

The crime seems too monstrous to contemplate. A six-year-old boy, accompanied by eight-year-old twin brothers, allegedly broke into an apartment, sought out a one-month-old baby, and punched, kicked, and beat the infant nearly to death.

Juveniles Are Committing More Violent Crimes

The baby survived but is expected to suffer permanent brain damage. The six-year-old, who reportedly said he wanted to kill the baby because the baby's parents had harassed him and looked at him the wrong way, has since been charged with assault and trespassing. The twins have each been charged with burglary.

The assault, which occurred in April 1996 in a run-down section of Richmond, California, is a shocking anomaly. It is unusual for children as young as six or eight to be charged with serious violent crimes. But some fear this may not be true for long. Recent studies indicate that juveniles are committing crimes at younger ages, and the crimes they commit are increasingly more violent.

In response to mounting public concern about this, state lawmakers have been rushing to pass legislation designed to crack down on juvenile lawbreakers with stiffer penalties for serious offenses. Proponents of these "get tough" measures argue that the juvenile justice system, with its focus on rehabilitation, is too soft on young offenders. Those opposed argue that tougher sanctions ignore the root cause of juvenile crime and will not curb the violence.

The sudden push for juvenile justice reform is being driven in part by alarming new statistics. Recent studies show that:

• while overall crime rates have decreased in recent years, juvenile arrest rates for violent crimes increased nearly 60 percent between 1983 and 1992;

• the number of juveniles arrested for murder tripled between 1984 and 1994;

• the juvenile arrest rate for weapons violations increased 75 percent between 1987 and 1992; and

• if current trends continue, juvenile arrests for violent crime are expected to double by 2010.

Experts disagree over what is fueling these statistics. Common theories range from the general—a widespread breakdown in social structure and family cohesiveness—to the specific—growing drug use among those under 18 and increased availability of guns on the street.

Some advocates of reform say the problem is simply that kids are no longer afraid of getting caught because the punishments meted out by juvenile judges are too lenient. Until recently, juvenile courts were charged with protecting delinquents as much as punishing them. Sentences, which often included counseling, focused more on reform than on retribution.

"Recent studies indicate that juveniles are committing crimes at younger ages, and the crimes they commit are increasingly more violent."

Created at the turn of the twentieth century, the juvenile justice system was founded on the theory that children are impressionable, more susceptible to change than adults. Special courts and detention facilities were established to rehabilitate young offenders. It was believed that with appropriate guidance youthful miscreants could be turned away from a life of crime.

Reform advocates say the system has failed to keep pace with the surge in violent offenders. They note that overburdened courts and detention facilities are often forced to confine juveniles for only short periods of time before turning them out on the street to commit more—and often even more violent—crimes. The system no longer works, critics say, because today's young offender has learned how to work the system.

Suggested Reforms of the Juvenile Justice System

In an effort to keep the most violent youths off the streets, several states have either passed or are considering laws that would lower the age at which juveniles could be tried as adults for certain crimes. In Wisconsin, for example, children as young as 10 can now be tried as adults for murder. Rather than spending just a few years in detention facilities, juveniles convicted of serious crimes in states that have passed these laws now face the same lengthy sentences that adults do.

Reforms like these have been sweeping the nation, according to Rich Gable, director of applied research at the National Center for Juvenile Justice in Pittsburgh. Since 1994, half the states have done something significant in the juvenile justice area, Gable said.

Some of the popular reform measures include:

• Allowing public access to juvenile court proceedings and records. Historically, juvenile hearings were closed and records were sealed to protect offenders from being branded as criminals for their youthful misdeeds.

• Implementing "three strikes" laws. Under these, juveniles arrested more than three times are automatically tried as adults.

• Holding parents legally responsible for their children's delinquent acts.

• Requiring convicted offenders to attend strict, military-style boot camps.

• Enforcing nighttime curfews for teens.

Critics of hard-line legal reforms claim that harsher penalties may only serve to make the problem worse and that the focus should be on preventive measures.

"There's no evidence that incarceration policies have any appreciable effect on crime rates," said University of Minnesota Law Professor Barry Feld. "If they did, since we've tripled our incarceration rate in the last decade and a half, we should be in a crime-free environment. And we're not," he said.

In fact, preliminary research indicates that making kids do hard time may only serve to make them hardened criminals. In a 1996 study, researchers [Charles E. Frazier et al.] in Florida found that a group of teens in that state who were tried and sentenced as adults had a higher tendency to commit more, and more serious, crimes once released than did kids who remained in the juvenile court system.

"At the very least," the study's authors wrote, "our findings clearly suggest that the 'get tough' message that transfer [to adult court] is designed to send to young offenders has little discernible deterrent effect."

Identifying and Prosecuting the Worst Juveniles

Nevertheless, tough sanctions are appropriate in some cases, according to Shay Bilchik, administrator of the Office of Juvenile Justice and Delinquency Prevention in Washington, D.C.

"We need to identify the most hardcore offenders and move them out of the juvenile system and prosecute them criminally," Bilchik said. "But we also need to make sure that this is done in a thoughtful and deliberate manner, not in a wholesale sweeping of kids out of the juvenile justice system. We have to treat each case individually and determine what each child needs."

"Reform advocates say the [juvenile justice] system has failed to keep pace with the surge in violent offenders."

To do just that, some states are combining traditional rehabilitation and "get tough" approaches with a strong emphasis on prevention and follow-up supervision. These so-called blended sentencing programs give juvenile judges discretion to sentence offenders to either juvenile or adult penalties. In some cases, an adult sentence is suspended as long as the offender meets certain criteria.

For example, Colorado's two-year-old Youth Offender System (YOS) offers a second chance to kids 14 to 18 who have been tried and sentenced in adult court. In return for suspended sentences, the kids endure several weeks of exercise and discipline in a juvenile boot camp, followed by counseling, education, and life-skills training. Kids who fail to respond must serve their adult sentences.

The program is too new to evaluate, said YOS Deputy Director Richard Swanson. "We've only had about five kids go through it. We think it will be 1998 or 1999 before we can determine a reasonable recidivism rate," he said.

Many critics of hard-line measures argue that prevention, not punishment, should be the aim of reform efforts. These experts cite studies showing that a child's exposure to poverty, family and community violence, and neglect and abuse greatly increases the likelihood the child will commit violent crimes.

> *"Critics of hard-line legal reforms claim that . . . the focus should be on preventive measures."*

"Solutions don't lie with the criminal justice system," Feld said, noting that "the biggest single indicator for youths at risk for committing crime is poverty." Rather than focusing on penalties, politicians should support programs like the minimum wage and universal health insurance, which would help impoverished families in child rearing, Feld said.

Breaking the cycle of violence is key to curbing the surge in teen crime, according to Bilchik. "Some children are exposed to multiple forms of violence in the home—they watch one parent abuse another or they are abused or neglected. This can have a tremendous impact on their chances of increased delinquency or violence later on," Bilchik said.

Prevention Programs

A prevention-focused pilot program in Orange County, California, which recently reported successful preliminary results, is being watched closely by experts across the country. The program targets first-time offenders who are deemed most likely to commit repeat offenses.

The kids are required to perform community service work under close supervision, and they and their families receive counseling and some financial help. According to initial reports, the rate of recidivism among program participants was about half that of a similar group of teens who did not participate.

Despite these hopeful early results, it may be years before it is clear whether programs like this or Colorado's YOS or the new tougher sanctions will have a lasting impact on youth crime. In the meantime, the debate over which approach works best is likely to continue.

Feld noted that the dispute boils down to a choice between dealing with social forces that put kids at risk and responding after the fact. You can address these issues long-term and preventively or in response to an acute crisis. The easiest way to think about this is, we either invest in Head Start or we have to build more prisons."

Tough Punishments Are Necessary to Prevent Juvenile Crime

by Woody West

About the author: *Woody West is associate editor of* Insight, *a weekly newsmagazine.*

Rarely do you hear the phrase "juvenile delinquency"—a term prevalent decades ago that signified worrisome but not cataclysmic behavior. As ever-younger predators not only violate personal safety and property rights and disregard moral standards, however, "delinquency" seems a quaint label.

An Emerging Consensus to Get Tough on Violent Juveniles

Homicide arrests among 14- to 17-year-olds have tripled during the last decade, for grotesque example, and that age group will expand by 20 percent during the next decade. There appears to be a fitful consensus emerging about how to handle these youthful raptors, but it is bitterly controversial.

Across the country, states are making drastic changes in handling juveniles. "The thrust of the new laws is to get more juveniles into the adult criminal-justice system," the *New York Times* reported recently with faint disapproval, "where they will presumably serve longer sentences under more punitive conditions."

The trend outrages liberals. "We are stepping down a very grim path toward eliminating childhood," frets Lisa Greer of the Los Angeles County Public Defender's Office. Her perspective is odd when you reflect that vicious crimes by teens contradict the meaning of "childhood" in any useful sense. Whether this brutality is due to the usually invoked factors—poverty, family disintegration, violence in the popular culture—is adjunctive, at least. Punishment is culturally imperative for those who murder, maim, rob, burglarize and terrorize.

A principal argument against consigning younger offenders to adult prison holds that incarceration is grad school for criminals. In Florida and New Jersey, studies supposedly have found a lower rate of subsequent offenses among those sentenced as juveniles than as adults. In both states, though, the comparisons cover a relatively short period since laws on sentencing were changed.

This is harsh business. But as a result of what has become a congenitally feeble juvenile criminal-justice system—to the extent that not even names, as a rule, can be made public in heinous crimes—the young have learned an ominous lesson: They can get away with breaking the law indefinitely with hardly a risk of swift, sure and stern punishment.

What are the alternatives? There are notions around—"home arrest" with electronic monitoring, for instance. Curfews are in fashion, as are programs to steer "at-risk" youngsters away from the precipice, a vague concept but perhaps with some merit. (What does a community do about a 6-year-old who batters a baby, as in the 1996 West Coast case? That's probably beyond remediation and can only be accommodated—if that's the word—by recognizing that evil exists.)

The boot-camp technique also is chic, the latest penalogical panacea despite no verdict on its efficacy. There are indications that it delivers less than hoped (Arizona dropped the program). Imposing a form of military discipline on first-time offenders for 90 days, with the prospect of probation rather than hard time if they "graduate," is fundamentally flawed, however politically appealing it may be.

> *"The young have learned an ominous lesson: They can get away with breaking the law indefinitely with hardly a risk of swift, sure and stern punishment."*

The Marine Corps (the pattern for the civilian boot camp) not only imposes implacable discipline, it enables recruits to become part of a tradition, to join a proud "little platoon," as it were. In addition, this cohesive code will be the standard for young troopers for the rest of their tour—rather than seeming a transient thing. Transgression is not winked at: The institutional adage goes that to err is human, to forgive divine—neither of which is Marine Corps policy.

Clearly, however, in the civil world there is sentiment for stouter bars and tougher terms for teenage criminals. Ernest Tubbs used to sing of a jailbird who lamented, "I'm alone and it's my shame, I'm a number not a name"—a sentiment that hardly would be understood in cell blocks today. That's part of the problem: The concept of shame largely has been jettisoned, as has its first cousin, humiliation.

The purposes of a criminal-justice system must be, in order of priority, to protect the public, to punish (for the sake of the criminal and for society's sense of moral equity), to deter and, if possible, to rehabilitate. The latter is an elusive concept. Likely, the most that can be done is to teach the thugs to read and write—which the public schools seem unable or unwilling to do—and get some of them to recognize that it's them who are out of step, not the rest of us.

Thorny thicket, to be sure. But what can be said bluntly is that when flood waters are ravaging, build the levees higher.

Both Prevention Programs and Punishment Are Needed to Control Juvenile Crime

by James Alan Fox

About the author: *James Alan Fox is dean of the College of Criminal Justice at Northeastern University in Boston. He is the author of* Trends in Juvenile Violence: Report to the United States Attorney General on Current and Future Trends in Juvenile Offending.

Judging from countless media reports in newspapers from coast to coast, it would surely seem that we have finally gotten a handle on the Nation's crime problem. The most recent FBI release of crime statistics for 1995 revealed a welcome drop in violent crime, including an 8 percent decline in homicide. After four straight years of lower crime levels, some crime experts and law enforcement officials have even dared boldly to suggest that we're winning the war against crime.

Declining Crime Rates but Rising Juvenile Crime Rates

Though recent trends are encouraging, at least superficially, there is little time to celebrate these successes. It is doubtful that today's improving crime picture will last for very long. Most likely, this is the calm before the crime storm. While many police officials can legitimately feel gratified about the arrested crime rate—better that it be down than up—there is much more to the great crime drop story. Hidden beneath the overall drop in homicide and other violent crime is a soaring rate of mayhem among teenagers.

There are actually two crime trends ongoing in America—one for the young and one for the mature, which are moving in opposite directions. Since 1990, for example, the rate of homicide committed by adults, ages 25 and older, has

From James Alan Fox, "Should the Federal Government Have a Major Role in Reducing Juvenile Crime? Pro," *Congressional Digest,* August/September 1996. Reprinted with permission from the author.

declined 18 percent as the baby boomers matured well past their crime prime years. At the same time, however, the homicide rate by teenagers, ages 14 to 17, has increased 22 percent. Even more alarming and tragic is that over the past decade, the homicide rate at the hands of teenagers has nearly tripled, increasing 172 percent from 1985 to 1994.

Therefore, while the overall U.S. homicide rate has indeed declined in recent years, the rate of juvenile murder continues to grow, unabated by the spread of community policing, increased incarceration, and a variety of other popular crime-fighting strategies. In the overall crime mix, the sharp decline in crime among the large adult population has eclipsed the rising crime rate among the relatively small population of teens.

> *"Hidden beneath the overall drop in homicide and other violent crime is a soaring rate of mayhem among teenagers."*

Trends in age-specific violent arrest rates for homicide, rape, robbery, and aggravated assault confirm the patterns found in homicide statistics. Teenagers now exceed all age groups, even young adults, in their absolute rate of arrest for violent crime overall. Conventional wisdom in criminology—that young adults generally represent the most violence-prone group—apparently needs to be modified in light of these disturbing changes.

Causes of the Youth Violence Wave

The causes of the surge in youth violence since the mid-1980s reach, of course, well beyond demographics. There have been tremendous changes in the social context of crime over the past decade, which explain why this generation of youth—the young and the ruthless—is more violent than others before it. Our youngsters have more dangerous drugs in their bodies, more deadly weapons in their hands, and a seemingly more casual attitude about violence. It is clear that too many teenagers in this country, particularly those in urban areas, are plagued with idleness and even hopelessness. A growing number of teens and preteens see few feasible or attractive alternatives to violence, drug use, and gang membership. For them, the American Dream is a nightmare. There may be little to live for and to strive for, but plenty to die for and even to kill for.

The problem of kids with guns cannot be overstated in view of recent trends in gun-related killings among youth. Since the mid-1980s, the number of gun-homicides—particularly with handguns—perpetrated by juveniles has quadrupled, while the prevalence of juvenile homicide involving all other weapons combined has remained virtually constant.

Guns are far more lethal in several respects. A 14-year-old armed with a gun is far more menacing than a 44-year-old with a gun. Although juveniles may be untrained in using firearms, they are more willing to pull the trigger over trivial matters—a leather jacket, a pair of sneakers, a challenging remark, or no reason at all—without fully considering the consequences. Also, the gun psychologi-

116

cally distances the offender from the victim; if the same youngster had to kill his or her victim (almost always someone known) with hands, he or she might be deterred by the physical contact.

The Breakdown of Family Structures

While the negative socializing forces of drugs, guns, gangs, and the media have become more threatening, the positive socializing forces of family, school, religion, and neighborhood have grown relatively weak and ineffective. Increasingly, children are being raised in homes disrupted by divorce and economic stress; too many children emerge undersocialized and undersupervised.

At this juncture, as many as 57 percent of children in America do not have full-time parental supervision, either living with a single parent who works full time or in a two-parent household with both parents working full time. The lack of parental supervision for young children is nearly as great. As many as 49 percent of children under age six do not have the benefit of full-time parenting. While some children enjoy suitable substitute supervision provided by friends and relatives or in day-care, far too many do not.

I do not mean to imply any special blame on the part of parents, and mothers in particular. While some parents are terribly ill prepared for the task of raising children, most parents are well meaning and would like to have a greater role in their children's lives. However, many families lack the support to control and guide their children. We should assist parents, not assail them.

The problem of unsupervised youth does not end nor the solution necessarily begin with the breakdown of the traditional family. Because of deep funding cuts in support programs for youth—from after-school care to recreation, from mentoring to education—as a society we are missing the fleeting opportunity to compensate for the diminished role of the family. As a consequence, children spend too little time engaged in structured activity with positive role models and too much time "hanging out" or watching a few

> *"Our youngsters have more dangerous drugs in their bodies, more deadly weapons in their hands, and a seemingly more casual attitude about violence."*

savage killings on television as after-school entertainment. Bored and idle, our children have just too much time to kill—perhaps literally.

Whoever called baby boomer parents the "permissive generation" hasn't been listening to the messages. We are constantly telling our kids, "Don't." "Don't do drugs." "Don't carry guns." "Don't have unsafe sex." "Don't watch Beavis and Butt-head." But what can they do? For the sake of short-term economic savings, we have closed down the neighborhood movie houses, community recreation centers, and local swimming pools. To control taxes, we have neglected the zoos, playgrounds, ball fields, and lakes. School districts everywhere have abandoned after-school activities and intramural sports.

117

The resulting problem of unsupervised youth is clearly reflected in the time-of-day patterns of juvenile violence. The prime time for juvenile crime is during the after-school hours—from 3 pm to 7 pm—and certainly not after midnight when curfew laws might be contemplated.

As if the situation with youth violence was not bad enough already, future demographics are expected to make matters even worse. Not only are today's violent teens maturing into more violent young adults, but they are being succeeded by a new and large group of teenagers. The same massive baby-boom cohort that as teenagers produced a crime wave in the 1970s has since grown up and had children of their own. There are now 39 million children in this country under the age of 10, more young children than at any time since the 1950s when the original baby boomers were in grade school. The newest group of youngsters—the baby boomerang cohort—will soon reach their adolescence.

A Future Crime Wave?

By the year 2005, the number of teens, ages 14 to 17, will swell by 17 percent, with an even larger increase among people of color—20 percent among African-Americans and 30 percent among Latinos. Given the difficult conditions in which many of these youngsters grow up—with inferior schools and violence-torn neighborhoods—many more teenagers will be at risk in the years ahead.

Tragically, the number of violent teens has grown in recent years, even as the population of teenagers has contracted. But the teen population has bottomed out and is now on the upswing. If current rates of offending remain unchanged, the number of teens who commit murder and other serious violent crimes shall increase, if only because of the demographic turnaround in the population at risk. However, given the worsening conditions in which children are being raised, given the breakdown of all our institutions as well as of our cultural norms, given our wholesale disinvestment in youth,

> *"Increasingly, children are being raised in homes disrupted by divorce and economic stress; too many children emerge undersocialized and undersupervised."*

our Nation faces the grim prospect of a future wave of juvenile violence that may make the 1990s look like "the good old days."

The hopeful news is that there is still time to stem the tide—to prevent the next wave of youth crime. But we must act now—by reinvesting in schools, recreation, job training, support for families, and mentoring. We must act now while this baby-boomerang generation is still young and impressionable, and will be impressed with what a teacher, a preacher, or some other authority figure has to say. If we wait until these children reach their teenage years and the next crime wave is upon us, it may be too late to do much about it.

The challenge for the future, therefore, is how best to deal with youth violence.

Unfortunately, we are obsessed with quick and easy solutions that will not work, such as the wholesale transfer of juveniles to the jurisdiction of the adult court, parental responsibility laws, midnight curfews, the V-chip, boot camps, three strikes, even caning and capital punishment, at the expense of long-term and difficult solutions that will work, such as providing young children with strong, positive role models, quality schools, and recreation programs.

Three Strikes Laws Will Not Work

One of the most compelling easy solutions is the "three strikes you're out" movement for repeat offenders that has swept across America, from Washington State, where it began, to Washington, D.C., where our congressmen and congresswomen are eager to show their constituents that they can strike out the side on crime.

Besides the significant drain on court resources as many more felons demand jury trials, disputing second and third strike calls more vociferously than Billy Martin ever did, besides the long-term effects of filling our prisons with aging lifers whose criminal history is really history, and besides the inevitable miscarriages of justice when certain petty felons get sent up the river inappropriately, why do we need this kind of automatic provision? Most States have long maintained a provision for

> *"Bored and idle, our children have just too much time to kill—perhaps literally."*

locking up the so-called "three-time losers." On a case-by-case basis, certain habitual offenders could and should be put on ice for an extended period of time. What's so wrong with discretion? Even in baseball, umpires have discretion in calling strikes. The umpire rules whether the pitch was on the corner or whether the batter checked his swing. Perhaps we should give judges as much discretion as the umps. Punishments should be based on the nature of the crimes, not the number.

The same concern over the elimination of judicial discretion applies to the national movement toward the automatic waiver of violent juveniles to the adult court. Undeniably, certain repeat violent juvenile offenders have demonstrated through recidivism that they are not amenable to treatment. These offenders can and should be transferred to the adult system. But this is not the case with all juvenile violent offenders, even though they may commit an adult-like crime such as murder or rape. The inspiration for their vicious crimes often stems from their immaturity—for example, kids committing murder in order to impress their peers.

Punishment or Prevention?

Don't misunderstand me. I'm not opposed to punishment (except capital punishment). However, we cannot deal effectively with teen violence through the threat of the criminal justice system. The threat of punishment, no matter how harsh, cannot deter kids who face the threat of violence every day in their class-rooms and their neighborhoods. As far as they are concerned, the criminal justice system can just take a number and wait its turn in line. Often these are juveniles who care little about the future, who don't expect to live past their 21st birthday. The prospect of a long-term prison sentence or even the death penalty will not dissuade them in the least.

> *"Our Nation faces the grim prospect of a future wave of juvenile violence that may make the 1990s look like 'the good old days.'"*

Of course, I am hardly the first person to advocate for prevention rather than punishment. Many policymakers have been pushing prevention programs—from education to recreation—but not always prevention that is early enough. For example, anti-violence curricula promoting conflict resolution skills have been introduced in many high schools across America. But that's far too little and much too late. Those teens whom we most need to reach are often not in high school. And if they are in high school, they're not listening. If they're listening, they don't care.

We must instead locate these programmatic efforts in the primary grades where we can make a significant difference in the attitudes and behaviors of children before they are seduced by the temptations of street thrills, gang membership, drugs, and crime. Of course, we then must be patient, for we will not see an impact of this investment on the crime problem for a number of years until these young children become teenagers and are not as violent as their predecessors.

From a purely political point of view, investing in long-term solutions may not seem overly attractive. Rather, the three R's of punishment—retribution, revenge, and retaliation—clearly tend to promote the fourth R, re-election. Nevertheless, it is critical that our leaders on Capitol Hill maintain a balanced view between punishment and prevention. As always, an ounce of prevention in terms of programs for youth is worth 10 years of cure inside the walls of a prison cell. It is far easier and considerably less expensive to build the child than to rebuild the adult criminal. With a Federal commitment to invest in long-term, workable solutions to the problem of youth crime, we can stem the tide of violence before it is too late.

Violence Prevention Programs Can Stop Juvenile Crime

by Mark H. Moore

About the author: *Mark H. Moore is the Guggenheim Professor in the John F. Kennedy School of Government at Harvard University.*

By all accounts, violent crimes—homicide, rape, robbery, aggravated assault—are on the decline in the United States. Even so, there is an important reason for society to be concerned: America is now experiencing a historically unprecedented epidemic of youth violence. Even as overall levels of violent crime have diminished over the last half decade, rates at which young people aged 14–18 have attacked and been victimized by one another have increased dramatically. Both offending and victimization rates for this age group are now at historical peaks.

Reasons for Concern

An important social-science finding of the last decade is that citizens' fears of crime are tied less closely to their objective risks of victimization than to far more common conditions such as abandoned vehicles, broken streetlights, littering, and graffiti. These are apparently interpreted as "signs of crime." One of the most important of such signs is "disorderly youth." Society has long viewed young males as generally threatening. Indeed, social psychologists have learned that they can induce uncomfortably high levels of fear simply by showing ordinary citizens still pictures of groups of young males walking toward them. Given that there are lots of kids, that they frequent subways, parks, and malls where many other citizens pass, it is easy to understand how youth violence would become a particularly scary problem for the society.

Youths, perceived as potentially violent offenders, are not only good at spreading the immediate fear of victimization; they are also good at sowing the seeds of despair and deep fears about the future as well as the present. When

From Mark H. Moore, "The Epidemic of Youth Violence," *Jobs & Capital*, Winter 1995. Reprinted by permission of the Milken Institute for Job and Capital Formation, Santa Monica, California.

13-year-olds kill one another, when 14- and 15-year-olds are recruited into drug-dealing gangs and asked to shoot competitors, much of the society feels ashamed as well as frightened. Where are the parents, people reasonably ask, where the schools, where the community associations that should be keeping these children on a far different path to adulthood?

> *"Young people are being killed, and their chances for a better life ruined by their own offenses."*

These are the broad reasons that society is, and should be, concerned about the epidemic of youth violence. Society should also be concerned, however, simply because young people are being killed, and their chances for a better life ruined by their own offenses. The nation is losing a generation of poor young men who, in an important sense, never had the chance that a decent democratic society should give to its youngest and poorest citizens.

Origins of the Problem

How did we arrive at this sad and dangerous condition? The story likely begins with the weakening of the economic and social infrastructure of some inner-city neighborhoods. The flight of middle-class residents of all races; the boarding up of many small businesses that had provided a social and economic anchor for the communities; the disappearance of relatively high-paying blue-collar jobs from surrounding areas; a decline in the quantity and quality of education, recreation, and other public services; a growth in teenage pregnancy and the failure of teenage fathers to provide for their children, etc., left some urban neighborhoods shorn of economic and social capital.

Such "blasted" neighborhoods are particularly bad for children, who must make the long, difficult transition from infancy to adulthood. I have elsewhere described this process as one that requires children to change from "defenseless barbarians" into "resourceful citizens." The move from "barbarian" to "citizen" is accomplished by helping children internalize social norms that should govern their behavior. Poor neighborhoods have often lacked the economic and social resources to provide either. Often, they can neither shower love on children nor equip them with the skills that would allow them to complete school and get a job. Nor can they muster the firmness and self-confidence required to keep children safe from their own risky behavior in the short run, and to develop a strong sense of moral responsibility over the long run. The result is that children fill the social void with gang membership. Once established, the influence of gangs has widened to include many children for reasons of self-defense, or the natural desire to be in style.

The Crack Cocaine Epidemic

Into this world, starting in 1985–87, came the "crack" epidemic. The crack tornado touched down in these blasted neighborhoods partly because the users were there. It also mattered, however, that the ordinary forces of social control were *not* there. The informal social control that could be exerted by neighborhood associations, churches, or simple fellowship was weak. Indeed, given the attractive economic opportunities associated with drug dealing, whatever informal institutions existed could easily have been overwhelmed or suborned by the economic power of the illegal supply system. Nor was formal public social control up to the task. There were too few police. And, as important, there was too weak a relationship between those who lived in and cared about the areas and the police who patrolled them.

The result of the crack epidemic was to further erode the basic social structures of these neighborhoods. Unlike the heroin epidemic of the late sixties and early seventies, the cocaine epidemic sucked women and, therefore, mothers into its vortex. The public response to the epidemic, when it came, swept many men off the streets into jails and prisons for long terms. With mothers disabled and fathers jailed, and the important economic opportunities centered on the drug trade, gangs (many now led and staffed by kids who had become 18–24 rather than 14–18) became even more powerful. To ensure their

> *"Children fill the social void with gang membership."*

survival and success, they armed themselves, and their gun battles took their toll not only among the combatants, but among innocent bystanders. America hadn't seen anything like this wave of violence since the thirties.

With such gangs so dominant, larger numbers of other less criminally inclined kids were forced for reasons of self-defense, or tempted for reasons of culture and style, to join or begin to look and act like gang members or drug dealers. They, too, took advantage of a plentiful supply of guns to arm themselves. Suddenly, their far more frequent minor quarrels became as deadly as the battles among the gangs and youthful drug dealers. The net result of these developments is the observed epidemic of youth violence.

The Future

The future does not look much better. Ten years ago [in 1985], demographers were predicting that society would now be enjoying a dramatic reduction in crime rates due to a decline in the number and proportion of teenagers and young men—representing the high crime years—in the general population. As noted above, we got that reduction. But its magnitude was reduced by dramatic increases in the crime rates of the smaller number of teenagers and young men. In the next five years [until the year 2000], the number and proportion of the young, urban, male population will grow rapidly as the "echo baby boom" works its way through school and the entry into the workplace. Many of these kids will have grown up in conditions that are, if anything, worse than the conditions their older brothers faced.

Of course, it may be that there are some self-limiting processes that will begin to operate to control this epidemic. It is possible that the pool of those "susceptible" to the allure of violence will dry up—that all the youths inclined in this direction will end up dead or in prison. More hopeful is the possibility that the concrete experience of seeing children die and attending funerals will begin to change attitudes among the children themselves and the communities in which they live. Out of the pain and despair will come a powerful social mobilization against violence by those most affected by it. In fact, there is a great deal of evidence to show that precisely such a mobilization is now occurring, and that communities are finding some capacity to respond to youth violence. To the extent that such a movement is occurring, it would be particularly important for any governmental response to aid rather than frustrate that response.

The Governmental Response

Still, it seems unlikely that these forces alone will be able to deal adequately with the future. Like it or not, government too will have to act to deal with the pain of the past and with the threat to the future. An important question is how.

Unfortunately, what government and public agencies can best do to deal with the epidemic of youth violence also remains unclear. For a while, we will have to be guided by plausible theories rather than demonstrated facts about what will work. Here are some principles that might usefully guide a serious public response to the epidemic.

First, it is important that society stay focused on the issue of youth violence and not let more generalized concerns about crime guide the public response. Strikingly little of the public discussion and governmental response focuses on the special problem of youth violence.

The things that are debated—capital punishment, "three strikes and you're out," an expanded federal jurisdiction, even the ban on assault weapons—have remarkably little connection to any plausibly effective attack on youth violence. Thus, much of our current discussion and policies are simply missing the core of the problem.

Second, in dealing with youth violence, we should divide the problem into at least three parts. One part is associated with youth involvement in illicit drug dealing. A second part is associated with gangs (that may or may not be involved in drug dealing). A third part involves youth who are not involved in drug dealing or gangs, but are carrying weapons and end up using them to settle relatively minor disputes.

Among these different components, the most difficult may be that linked to illicit drug trafficking. Society

> *"The result of the crack epidemic was to further erode the basic social structures of these neighborhoods."*

may well gain some benefits from making drugs such as heroin and cocaine illegal. But it is also true that society pays a price for such policies, and part of the price is an increase in violence associated with illicit trafficking. It is not exactly clear what kinds of police practices or sentencing policies could effectively reduce the violence associated with illicit trafficking while keeping the trafficking illegal. Perhaps trafficking violence could trigger aggressive police patrol and enhanced investigative efforts in neighborhoods. Perhaps use of youth in drug trafficking, and particularly in violence related to drug trafficking, could carry especially heavy penalties.

The Problem of Gangs

Dealing effectively with gang violence may also prove difficult. One major difficulty is that society and the police may have to recognize a great deal of heterogeneity among gangs. The worst gangs—those that are large, durable, well-armed, involved in drug dealing, aggressive, active in recruiting new blood, skillful in shaping new kids to the demands of crime and violence, etc.— may be relatively rare. Many other gangs may represent much less of a threat.

Once the gangs are accurately characterized, the strategies for dealing with them will become more obvious. With respect to the worst gangs, it will be important to find ways to weaken them. Arresting the leaders and the "shooters" may be important, though there is the risk that prison will simply delay rather than reduce the violence, and that the violence will recur once they return to the streets. Finding ways to weaken their ability to recruit new members by making gang member-

> *"Strikingly little of the public discussion and governmental response focuses on the special problem of youth violence."*

ship less attractive and less necessary may also be important. For example, gang members could be subject to restraining orders that curtail their movements and associations. Violations could be punished with visible and humiliating punishments such as doing menial but socially valuable work in the neighborhoods. With respect to gangs less committed to violent criminality, it may be possible to use them for more socially productive purposes. After all, the difference between a gang, a basketball league, and a boy scout troop may lie only in the values and purposes of its leadership, and the activities that the group engages in. In any case, it might be important to reduce the influence of all gangs by improving security in and on the way to schools so that youth are not forced to join gangs for self-defense, and by providing other recreational and social opportunities for gang "wannabes" and their friends.

With respect to the violence involving kids who are not drug dealers or gang members, it is probably important to take steps to reduce their access to firearms, and to teach alternative methods of resolving disputes. Such programs can be school-based in cities where much of the young population is in school. In areas where that is not true, it will be important to find wider platforms from which to reach out.

Finally, some broad preventive approaches hold some potential. It may turn out to be very important to reduce the number of kids who are inclined toward violence by reducing the violence that occurs in families either in front of children or against the children. Ways well short of weapons bans may also be found to reduce the availability and carrying of weapons among children. And there is much to be said for the utility of helping poor neighborhoods rebuild, both economically and socially.

Challenges to Bureaucracies and Politics

Note that to be able to actually implement such strategies, a great deal of pressure must be exerted on public institutions. Instead of reacting to violent crimes with standard, universal responses such as arrest and prosecution, police must shift to pro-active efforts to prevent violence and reduce fear through tailored, problem-solving interventions. Instead of processing cases involving youth and family violence as special kinds of crime, the juvenile court must find ways to use its powers to oversee families and others who care for children to help construct the missing structures of care, supervision and discipline that every child needs.

> *"Finding ways to weaken [gangs'] ability to recruit new members by making gang membership less attractive and less necessary may also be important."*

Equally important, our political discourse about the problem of violence must change. The false distinction between governmental agency on the one hand and community on the other must be abandoned in favor of recognition that all government agencies must become community agencies. So must the false distinction between public efforts to provide services and to hold citizens accountable be erased. In rebuilding blasted communities to save children's lives, the central challenge is for society to find ways to use public agencies to prime the pump of private capacity, and to combine assistance to citizens with enforceable public obligations.

Harsh Punishments for Juveniles Are Not Justified

by Franklin E. Zimring

About the author: *Franklin E. Zimring is a professor of law at the University of California, Berkeley.*

You can get dizzy these days listening to the statistics and studies being issued about crime. On one hand, rates of crime are down modestly in most places and way down in some cities like New York. On the other hand, public anxiety remains very high. There are special efforts to focus citizen fear on projected increases in youth crime in the United States over the next ten to fifteen years. Early in 1996 the Washington-based Council on Crime in America issued a report on crime warning of "a coming storm of juvenile violence." The House subcommittee on crime has just concluded a five-city road show on the prospects for a youth crime wave in the near future.

Predictions of a Future Juvenile Crime Wave

The biggest numbers and most specific policy recommendations on this pending juvenile crime wave come from Princeton professor and Brookings Institution fellow John DiIulio, who wrote in February 1996 that "about 270,000 more juvenile super-predators," will be roaming the streets of America by 2010 than were present in 1990. In "How to Stop the Coming Crime Wave," Professor DiIulio tells us there is a need for at least 150,000 new placements in juvenile secure confinement in the next 5 to 7 years alone. . . .

It turns out, however, that the DiIulio projections are phony for two reasons. The phrase "juvenile super-predator," is meaningless. And his "270,000 extra" such mythical creatures by 2010 can only be correct if infants or toddlers start committing armed robbery.

For starters, the term "super-predators" has never been defined. But we do know what a juvenile super-predator isn't. It is not a juvenile killer, nor a rapist, nor a habitual armed robber—the numbers on all these categories of offenders are vastly smaller than 270,000 and not likely to grow much. Instead, when

From Franklin E. Zimring, "Desperadoes in Diapers?" *Overcrowded Times*, August 1996. Reprinted by permission of the *Overcrowded Times*.

asked the basis for this number, Professor DiIulio notes that a series of studies have shown that about 6 percent of all boys are responsible for about half of all police contacts under age 18 in criminological studies of city youth populations. In the most important cohort study in Philadelphia, this 6 percent were classified as chronic delinquents because they had five or more police contacts for any cause. Some of these Philadelphia kids had committed violent acts: many had not. Most of the offenses committed by this 6 percent were not serious by any measure. In other cohort study settings like Racine, Wisconsin, the 6 percent of a youth cohort sample that was responsible for the majority of all police contacts in the study committed practically no life-threatening violence. DiIulio's assumption is that 6 percent of any population of young males are an imminent danger to the public. No study of any youth population supports that projection of predatory violence. Only if "super-predators" are people who do no more than shoplift and play hooky can the measurements of cohort studies lend any support to a 6 percent claim.

How Many Juvenile Criminals Will There Be?

But once this definition of super-predator is known, the arithmetic for a projection of 270,000 extra super-predators on our streets is astonishingly simple. DiIulio tells us that the number of boys under 18 in the United States is expected to expand from 32 million to 36.5 over the next 14 years. By assuming that serious delinquencies will be committed by 6 percent of that population, he finds an extra 270,000 super-predators by multiplying the additional 4.5 million male children under 18 by 0.06.

But this is hogwash. If 6 percent of all males under 18 are super-predators, that means we currently have over 1.9 million juvenile super-predators on our streets (32 million boys x .06 = 1,920,000). We would hardly notice another 270,000 by 2010. But the total estimate of current super-predators we obtain by this method is about twice as many as the total number of delin-

> *"The phrase 'juvenile super-predator' is meaningless."*

quents processed in juvenile court last year for anything at all. The reason for this huge overestimate of repeat delinquencies is simple. Most of the super-predators in DiIulio's formulation don't commit crimes.

What makes the DiIulio projection so bizarre is the assumption that children of all ages under 18 are dangerously crime prone. But it turns out that 93 percent of all juvenile arrests for violence occur after age 13. Young kids just don't commit crimes. Yet a larger percentage of Professor DiIulio's super-predators will be under age 6 in 2010 than over age 13. Over half the people he projects as candidates for confinement in the year 2010 will not be 9 years old. As many projected super-predators will be under age 3 as over age 15 in that year. At Princeton they are worried about desperadoes in diapers.

After a moment's thought, two-year-old super-predators in 2010 are less plausible than large green men from Mars. But the point worth examining is that nobody seems to have given these numbers even five minutes of scrutiny. . . . Indeed, there are incentives to come up with dramatic numbers for sound bites on the evening news, and no questioning of numbers as long as an academic projection fits the ideological preferences of its audience. Such a market for junk data will bring out the Lyndon LaRouche in lots of folks.

Politics and the Juvenile Crime Wave

The ideological needs of the moment seem to be for a youth crime wave set in the future so that government can shadow box against it by getting tough on juvenile crime in advance. It's a "heads-I-win, tails-you-lose" situation for the crime wave alarmists: They were right if crime rates go up; their policies can also be said to succeed even if the crime wave never happens. There are more than a few parallels here with the domestic scare about Communists in the late 1940s and early 1950s. If we find any Communists hiding under our beds, the alarm was justified. If there are no Communists under the bed, then the vigilance of citizens has saved the day.

> *"What makes the DiIulio projection so bizarre is the assumption that children of all ages under 18 are dangerously crime prone."*

The most frightening part of the saga of the super-predator is not the faulty arithmetic and conceptual sloppiness that produced the projections. Imaginary numbers are not rare in Washington these days. But this episode bears witness to a complete lack of quality control that afflicts contemporary debate on criminal justice policy. If politicians and analysts can believe "super-predator" toddlers, they can believe anything.

Prevention Efforts Should Be Aimed at Adult Violence

by Michael A. Males

About the author: *Michael A. Males, a doctoral student at the University of California, Irvine, is the author of* The Scapegoat Generation: America's War on Adolescents.

When a 3-year-old Los Angeles girl was murdered in an apparent gang killing in 1995, nationwide media coverage exploded. When a 3-year-old Beverly Hills boy was murdered by his 37-year-old father three weeks later, notice was scant. Two tragic killings of small children. One cited as the signature of today's brutal young, the other relatively ignored.

Hype over Juvenile Crime

Candidates of both parties and experts of all stripes proclaim skyrocketing violence among America's youth as the nation's most urgent crisis. Images of "children killing children" and "kids more violent at younger ages" grip the national psyche. Candidates compete to be tougher on teen crime. Experts declare the rise in youth violence to be all the more baffling and frightening because adult crime has not increased.

Ignored in the furor is that California—particularly Los Angeles—displays a stunningly different pattern, one that challenges conventional wisdom. The state's violent-crime increase in the last decade has centered not on teenagers, but on adults older than 30. Our grade-school kids are less violent today than at any time in the last 15 years. Since 1990, violent felony (including murder) rates have fallen among all age groups—particularly L.A. adolescents.

California's violent criminals are getting older. In 1955, the average age of violent arrestees was 28, up from 25 in 1985. From 1985 to 1995, the violent-crime arrest rate per capita among teens rose by 40%. But violent-crime rates

From Michael A. Males, "The Truth About Crime: Myth of Teenage Violence vs. Real Adult Menace," editorial, *Los Angeles Times*, September 15, 1996. Reprinted by permission of the author.

rose by 50% among 20- to 29-year-olds, 111% among those in their 30s, and 114% among those older than 40. In 1995, 45,000 Californians in their 30s were arrested for violence, more than those age 10 to 19.

The concurrent explosion in serious assaults by older California adults—39,000 in 1985, 107,000 in 1995—is what is driving the state's violence increase. As L.A. Police Det. Craig Rhody said, "Assault with a deadly weapon is a murder that just didn't happen" due to "luck or fate." State and national figures indicate much of the rising adult violence is directed at children and youths.

Crime Rates Driven Up by Adult Violence Against Children

In February 1996, the U.S. Department of Justice reported that nine of 10 murdered children (under age 12), and six in 10 murdered teens (age 12 to 17), are killed by grown-ups, not by other "children." In the last decade, the rate of "adults killing children" has increased by 50%. Many who deplored the 330,000 felony and misdemeanor violence arrests of youths in 1993 expressed no similar alarm about the 370,000 substantiated violent and sexual abuses of youths inflicted by their parents.

In California, domestic violence represents the largest single category of weapons-related crime. In the Los Angeles area, officers responded to a record-high 88,000 domestic-violence calls involving weapons in 1994. Children are far more likely to be household-violence victims than adults. A 1994 Department of Justice study found parents murder teenage children six times more often than the other way around. Especially troubling figures from the U.S. Advisory Board on Child Abuse and Neglect and the Centers for Disease Control show that a youth is a dozen times safer from being murdered at school, around hundreds of peers, than at home with a couple of grown-ups.

How, then, does the public get the idea that kids—who account for just 14% of violent crime arrests in California—represent an apocalyptic menace? Part of the problem is media sensationalizing. Recent studies by Berkeley researchers found that two-thirds of California's big-city broadcast-news stories on violence involved youths. Newspapers and magazines are also brimming with "teenage mayhem" stories.

"[California's] violent-crime increase in the last decade has centered not on teenagers, but on adults older than 30."

No wonder a 1994 Gallup poll concluded "because of recent news coverage of violent crimes committed by juveniles, the public has a greatly inflated view of the amount of violent crime committed by people under the age of 18." That survey found the average adult believes that youths commit 43% of all violent crime, three times the true number.

One can expect psychologists and police officers, who often rely on personal experiences and anecdotal evidence concerning troubled youths, to brand today's kids as uniquely scary. Last week's appalling crime is always scarier than 10 appalling crimes of 10 years ago. It is scholars and agency officials who should be analyzing trends and supplying context to the youth-violence debate. Instead, they often fan the hysteria.

Accurate Statistics on Youth Violence

Consider these myth-busting facts revealed in the California Department of Justice's annual "Crime & Delinquency in California" reports and 1995 county crime updates:

• Teenage and adult violence show identical trends, rising and falling in tandem statewide and in major counties.

• Youths show the largest decline of any age group in violent crime between 1990 and 1995, following a large increase in the late 1980s. From 1985 to 1990, violence arrests rose 75% among youths (defined by the department as age 10 to 17) and 63% among adults (age 18 to 69) in the five-county Los Angeles metropolitan area. Then, from 1990 to 1995, violent-crime rates declined 21% among L.A. youths and 13% among adults. The largest decline was in murders by youths, which fell from 407, in 1990, to 262, in 1995. By 1995, violence rates for youths and adults were identical.

> *"Nine of 10 murdered children (under age 12), and six in 10 murdered teens (age 12 to 17), are killed by grown-ups, not by other 'children.'"*

• Children's violent crimes are rarer and less serious today than at any time since 1979, when statistics on young children's crimes were first published. Arrests of children under 10 for violent crimes fell 40% from 1985 to 1995.

These statistics do not usually accompany the rising drumbeat among authorities and the media about "adolescent super-predators." Accordingly, politicians from President Bill Clinton to California Atty. Gen. Dan Lungren call for such get-tough approaches as curfew and truancy enforcement.

Yet, examination of crime trends in California's 12 most populous counties over the last decade shows no relation between tough police efforts against juveniles and youth crime. In particular, well-publicized police crackdowns in San Diego and San Jose met with higher-than-expected levels of youth crime. As University of Southern California (USC) sociologist Malcolm Klein recently concluded from 35 years of research on gangs, law-enforcement strategies have little to do with violence cycles.

The Campaign Against Youth

A nation whose top political leaders are engaged in a relentless campaign to scapegoat its own young for a complex array of social problems is suffering a fundamental crisis of accountability. In today's politically charged atmosphere, where interest groups wage anti-youth scare campaigns to win funding, then switch gears and rush to grab credit for any positive trends, reasoned analysis becomes impossible. The United States is increasingly unable to respond to even basic threats to its young people—especially when those threats stem from adult behaviors impolitic to confront.

The rise in youth violence, particularly murder, has occurred among minority populations and appears to stem from increasing youth poverty. The larger increase in middle-aged violence, evident among all races, is harder to explain, since this age group has become wealthier and more comfortable. Increased adult violence may be linked to another crisis not often discussed: The enormous rise in middle-aged drug abuse, reflected in a fourfold increase in deaths and a tripling in hospital emergencies among California 35- to 60-year-olds from overdoses of heroin, cocaine and prescription drugs in the last 15 years.

> *"The average adult believes that youths commit 43% of all violent crime, three times the true number."*

If California and the nation face a violent future, it is not due to some mythical teenage menace, but the personal misbehavior, economic abuses and official indifference inflicted by older generations that seem not to care what happens to the young.

Bibliography

Books

David C. Anderson — *Crime and the Politics of Hysteria: How the Willie Horton Story Changed American Justice.* New York: Random House, 1995.

D.A. Andrews and James Bonta — *The Psychology of Criminal Conduct.* Cincinnati: Anderson Publishing, 1994.

William J. Bennett, John J. DiIulio Jr., and John P. Walters — *Body Count: Moral Poverty . . . and How to Win America's War Against Crime and Drugs.* New York: Simon & Schuster, 1996.

Robert James Bidinotto, ed. — *Criminal Justice? The Legal System Versus Individual Responsibility.* Irvington, NY: Foundation for Economic Education, 1995.

James Ellroy — *My Dark Places: An L.A. Crime Memoir.* New York: Knopf, 1996.

Mansfield B. Frazier — *From Behind the Wall: Commentary on Crime, Punishment, and the Underclass by a Prison Inmate.* New York: Paragon House, 1995.

Kathlyn Taylor Gaubatz — *Crime in the Public Mind.* Ann Arbor: University of Michigan Press, 1995.

Diana R. Gordon — *The Return of the Dangerous Classes.* New York: Norton, 1994.

Edward Humes — *No Matter How Loud I Shout: A Year in the Life of Juvenile Court.* New York: Simon & Schuster, 1996.

Wendy Kaminer — *It's All the Rage: Crime and Culture.* Reading, MA: Addison-Wesley, 1995.

George L. Kelling and Catherine M. Coles — *Fixing "Broken Windows": Restoring Order in America's Cities.* Westport, CT: Praeger, 1995.

Mike A. Males — *The Scapegoat Generation: America's War on Adolescents.* Monroe, ME: Common Courage Press, 1996.

June Stephenson — *Men Are Not Cost-Effective: Male Crime in America.* New York: HarperPerennial, 1995.

134

Bibliography

Sanford Strong	*Strong on Defense: Survival Rules to Protect You and Your Family from Crime.* New York: Pocket Books, 1996.
Andrew Peyton Thomas	*Crime and the Sacking of America: The Roots of Chaos.* Washington, DC: Brassey's, 1994.
Willie L. Williams and Bruce B. Henderson	*Taking Back Our Streets: Fighting Crime in America.* New York: Scribner, 1996.
Franklin E. Zimring and Gordon Hawkins	*Crime Is Not the Problem: Lethal Violence in America.* New York: Oxford University Press, 1997.
Franklin E. Zimring and Gordon Hawkins	*Incapacitation: Penal Confinement and the Restraint of Crime.* New York: Oxford University Press, 1995.

Periodicals

Michael Castleman	"Opportunity Knocks," *Mother Jones,* May/June 1995.
Alexander Cockburn	"The War on Kids," *Nation,* June 3, 1996.
Charles Colson	"Why Not Commit a Crime?" *Christianity Today,* January 9, 1995.
Congressional Digest	"Juvenile Crime: 1996–97 Policy Debate Topic," August/September 1996.
Nick DiSpoldo	"Three-Strikes Laws: Cruel and Unusual?" *Commonweal,* June 14, 1996.
D. Stanley Eitzen	"Violent Crime: Myths, Facts, and Solutions," *Vital Speeches of the Day,* May 15, 1995.
Patrick Fagan	"The Real Root Cause of Violent Crime," *Vital Speeches of the Day,* December 15, 1995.
T. Markus Funk	"Young and Arrestless," *Reason,* February 1996.
David Gergen	"Taming Teenage Wolf Packs," *U.S. News & World Report,* March 25, 1996.
Henry A. Giroux	"Beating Up on Kids," *Z Magazine,* July/August 1996.
Malcolm Gladwell	"The Tipping Point," *New Yorker,* June 3, 1996.
Richard Lacayo	"Law and Order," *Time,* January 15, 1996.
Mike Males and Faye Docuyanan	"Crackdown on Kids: Giving Up on the Young," *Progressive,* February 1996.
Paul J. McNulty	"Natural Born Killers?" *Policy Review,* Winter 1995.
Salim Muwakkil	"Dead Wrong," *In These Times,* October 3, 1994.
Anthony M. Platt	"Crime Rave," *Monthly Review,* June 1995.
Paul H. Robinson	"Moral Credibility and Crime," *Atlantic Monthly,* March 1995.
Bruce Shapiro	"How the War on Crime Imprisons America," *Nation,* April 22, 1996.

Crime

James Traub	"The Criminals of Tomorrow," *New Yorker*, November 4, 1996.
James Traub	"New York Story," *New Republic*, January 27, 1997.
James Q. Wilson	"What to Do About Crime," *Vital Speeches of the Day*, April 1, 1995.
Mortimer B. Zuckerman	"Scary Kids Around the Corner," *U.S. News & World Report*, December 4, 1995.

Organizations to Contact

The editors have compiled the following list of organizations concerned with the issues debated in this book. The descriptions are derived from materials provided by the organizations. All have publications or information available for interested readers. The list was compiled on the date of publication of the present volume; names, addresses, phone and fax numbers, and e-mail/Internet addresses may change. Be aware that many organizations take several weeks or longer to respond to inquiries, so allow as much time as possible.

American Civil Liberties Union (ACLU)
125 Broad St.
New York, NY 10004-2400
(212) 944-9800
fax: (212) 869-9065
Internet: http://www.aclu.org

The ACLU is a national organization that works to defend Americans' civil rights as guaranteed by the U.S. Constitution. It opposes curfew laws for juveniles and seeks to protect the right of gang members to assemble in public. Among the ACLU's numerous publications are the book *In Defense of American Liberties: A History of the ACLU,* the handbook *The Rights of Prisoners: A Comprehensive Guide to the Legal Rights of Prisoners Under Current Law,* and the briefing paper "Crime and Civil Liberties."

Cato Institute
1000 Massachusetts Ave. NW
Washington, DC 20001
(202) 842-0200
fax: (202) 842-3490
e-mail: cato@cato.org
Internet: http://www.cato.org

The Cato Institute is a libertarian public policy research foundation. It evaluates government policies and offers reform proposals in its publication *Policy Analysis.* Topics include "Crime, Police, and Root Causes" and "Prison Blues: How America's Foolish Sentencing Policies Endanger Public Safety." In addition, the institute publishes the bimonthly newsletter *Cato Policy Report* and the triannual *Cato Journal.*

Center for the Study of Youth Policy
University of Pennsylvania School of Social Work
4200 Pine St., 2nd Fl.
Philadelphia, PA 19104-4090
(215) 898-2229
fax: (215) 573-2791

The center studies issues concerning juvenile justice and youth corrections. It publishes the booklets *Home-Based Services for Serious and Violent Juvenile Offenders, Youth Violence: An Overview,* and *Meditation Involving Juveniles: Ethical Dilemmas and Policy Questions.*

Friends Outside National Organization
3031 Tisch Way, Suite 507
San Jose, CA 95128
(408) 985-8807
fax: (408) 985-8839
e-mail: jdy@aol.com

The organization works to break the cycle of crime and delinquency by addressing the factors that cause violence—child and spousal abuse, dependency on the welfare system, and the criminal lifestyle. It provides pre- and post-release assistance to offenders in an attempt to combat the high recidivism rate among ex-convicts. It publishes information on the organization and its services.

Heritage Foundation
214 Massachusetts Ave. NE
Washington, DC 20002
phone and fax: (202) 546-8328
Internet: http://www.heritage.org

The Heritage Foundation is a conservative public policy research institute. It advocates tougher sentencing and the construction of more prisons as means to reduce crime. The foundation publishes the quarterly journal *Policy Review,* which occasionally contains articles addressing juvenile crime.

Justice Fellowship
PO Box 16069
Washington, DC 20041-6069
(703) 904-7312
fax: (703) 478-9679
Internet: http://www.pfm.org/jf.htm

The Justice Fellowship is a national justice reform organization that advocates victims' rights, alternatives to prison, and community involvement in the criminal justice system. It aims to make the criminal justice system more consistent with biblical teachings on justice. It publishes the brochures *A Case for Victims' Rights* and *Beyond Crime and Punishment: Restorative Justice* as well as the quarterly newsletter *Justice Report.*

National Council on Crime and Delinquency (NCCD)
685 Market St., Suite 620
San Francisco, CA 94105
(415) 896-6223
fax: (415) 896-5109
e-mail: nccd@hooked.net
Internet: http://www.cascomm.com/users/nccd/

The NCCD is composed of corrections specialists and others interested in the juvenile justice system and the prevention of crime and delinquency. It advocates community-based treatment programs rather than imprisonment for delinquent youths. It opposes placing minors in adult jails and executing those who commit capital offenses before the age of eighteen. The NCCD publishes the quarterly *Crime and Delinquency* as well as the policy papers "Juvenile Justice Policy Statement" and "Unlocking Juvenile Corrections: Evaluating the Massachusetts Department of Youth Services."

National Crime Prevention Council (NCPC)
1700 K St. NW, 2nd Fl.
Washington, DC 20006-3817

(202) 466-6272
fax: (202) 296-1356
Internet: http://www.ncpc.org

The NCPC advocates job training and recreation programs as means to reduce youth crime and violence. The council provides training and technical assistance to groups and individuals interested in crime prevention and sponsors the Take a Bite out of Crime campaign. It publishes the book *Preventing Violence: Program Ideas and Examples,* the booklet *How Communities Can Bring Up Youth Free from Fear and Violence,* and the newsletter *Catalyst,* which is published ten times a year.

National Criminal Justice Association (NCJA)
444 N. Capitol St. NW, Suite 618
Washington, DC 20001
(202) 347-4900
fax: (202) 508-3859

The NCJA is an association of state and local police chiefs, judges, attorneys, and other criminal justice officials that seeks to improve the administration of state criminal and juvenile justice programs. It publishes the monthly newsletter *Justice Bulletin.*

National Criminal Justice Reference Service (NCJRS)
PO Box 6000
Rockville, MD 20849-6000
(800) 851-3420 (within the U.S.)
(301) 251-5500 (outside the U.S.)
e-mail: askncjrs@ncjrs.aspensys.com
Internet: http://www.ncjrs.org

The National Criminal Justice Reference Service is a clearinghouse that provides criminal justice information to professionals, practitioners, administrators, policy makers, and the general public. It publishes an electronic newsletter twice a week at the following address: listproc@ncjrs.aspensys.com.

National School Safety Center (NSSC)
4165 Thousand Oaks Blvd., Suite 290
Westlake Village, CA 91362
(805) 373-9977

Part of Pepperdine University, the center studies school crime and violence, including gang violence and hate crimes, and provides technical assistance to local school systems. The NSSC believes that teacher training is an effective way of reducing juvenile crime. It publishes the booklet *Gangs in Schools: Breaking Up Is Hard to Do* and the *School Safety Update Newsletter,* published nine times a year.

Office of Juvenile Justice and Delinquency Prevention (OJJDP)
633 Indiana Ave. NW
Washington, DC 20531
(202) 307-5911
fax: (202) 307-2093
Internet: http://www.ncjrs.org/ojjhome.htm

The OJJDP is a federal agency that monitors and works to improve the juvenile justice system. Among its goals are the prevention and control of illegal drug use and crime by juveniles. Through its Juvenile Justice Clearinghouse, the OJJDP distributes fact sheets and reports such as "How Juveniles Get to Criminal Court," "Gang Suppression and Intervention: Community Models," and "Minorities and the Juvenile Justice System."

Sentencing Project
918 F St. NW, Suite 501
Washington, DC 20004
(202) 628-0871
fax: (202) 628-1091
e-mail: staff@sproject.com
Internet: http://www.sproject.com

The project provides public defenders and other public officials with information on establishing and improving alternative sentencing programs that provide convicted persons with positive and constructive options to incarceration. It promotes increased public understanding of the sentencing process and alternative sentencing programs. It publishes the reports "Americans Behind Bars: A Comparison of International Rates of Incarceration," "Americans Behind Bars: One Year Later," and "Young Black Men and the Criminal Justice System: A Growing National Problem."

Violence Policy Center
1350 Connecticut Ave. NW, Suite 825
Washington, DC 20036
(202) 822-8200
Internet: http://www.vpc.org

The center is an educational foundation that conducts research on firearm violence, works to educate the public concerning the dangers of guns, and supports gun-control measures. The center's publications include the book *Cease-Fire: A Comprehensive Strategy to Reduce Firearms Violence* and the monthly on-line newsletter *VPC*.

Youth Crime Watch of America (YCWA)
S. Dadeland Blvd., Suite 100
Miami, FL 33156
(305) 670-2409
fax: (305) 670-3805
e-mail: ycwa@ycwa.org
Internet: http://www.ycwa.org

Youth Crime Watch of America strives to give youths the tools and guidance necessary to actively reduce crime and drug use in their schools and communities. Its publications include *Talking to Youth About Crime Prevention,* the workbook *Community-Based Youth Crime Watch Program Handbook,* and the motivational video *A Call for Young Heroes.*

Index

Crime

Index